What Readers

"I know deep in my heart that the *One With God* books are intended for me. They are my exclusive study now. Although I've read them several times, the words still provide profound meaning with the strengthening view of understanding. The Holy Spirit, through you, is taking me along my path more assuredly."
— Brenda K.

"These books are touching me, changing me, teaching me . . . beyond anything I could tell you."
— Kathie A.

"After studying *A Course in Miracles* for many years, I find the *One With God* books are helping to take me further toward a direct experience of the Holy Spirit's Presence within. In that sense, I see the books as a continuation of the *Course's* teachings."
— Noah B.

"Every time I read an excerpt from *One With God* I am reminded of what we are really about. Your awakening, Margie, is evident, and truly helps the readers on their path."
— Marcia M.

"I get emotional just thinking about how much these books have assisted my awakening. Thanks for your courage and candor. I am so grateful."
— Moira B.

ONE WITH GOD

ONE WITH GOD:

Awakening Through the Voice of the Holy Spirit

Book 4

Marjorie Tyler
Joann Sjolander
Margaret Ballonoff

One With God:
Awakening Through the Voice of the Holy Spirit

Book 4

ISBN: 978-0-9965785-8-5
ISBN: 0-996578587
Library of Congress Control Number: 2018947995

Cover and text design: Miko Radcliffe

Sacred Life Publishers™
SacredLife.com
Printed in the United States of America

Contents

Contents

Contents

The Final Release

Every thought that is not of kindness
is a reason to call on Me.

January 1, 2014

Good morning, Holy Spirit, and Happy New Year. I am happy to begin this New Chapter with You as my Sole Navigator. Thank You for the blessing of bringing me this far in the knowing of You as all there is. I look forward to the time when we will be fully joined, operating as One Self. What is Your instruction? You feel united with Me today in heart and mind, happy to be serving our purpose with the books, happy for all your many selves in the mind who are out pictured in the world of form. This is a time of celebration. You have completed scribing the first three books in our series. Yes, the books are ours because we are One. Their completion has been a joined effort along with Meera and Jo. You three now get to look back to the beginning and see how far you have come. Yes, My promise that "a book would be written" has been fulfilled. Each book has served your awakening, as well as the awakening of all in the one mind. You trust what I say is true, that it is to serve your growth, moment by moment. I am you, and you are Me. This Oneness is inclusive of all humanity. That will be understood more fully in the next phase of our work. We will proceed with the theme of the final release of attachment to the ego thought system.

Last night, mt had a dream about being swayed by a character who was finely dressed as a slick salesman in a large department store where she had bought some ceramic tableware. Mt already had all the dishes she wanted but had wandered back into the store because she was told of a sale. The salesman then handed her a fancy brochure and began his lecture on the advantages of buying more. She didn't understand why he was holding up a line of waiting customers just to talk to her. Mt did not really have an interest in buying more but stood and listened, thinking he liked her and was trying to be helpful.

When you awoke from the dream, you realized the salesman symbolized the ego, and that you were looking at your last attachments to the appearance of form. You could tell by his perfect presentation and garb that he was just a figure of your imagination but then realized there is still something in mt being called to play the ego's game. She is yet attracted to the special forms that give her pleasure in the world, but she also knows when she has had enough of it and can leave the showroom.

This is the stage where the three of you now stand with Me. You see the whole ego drama and know where you tend to fall for the sales pitch. This discernment will sharpen rapidly so that saying no to the ego will be easy, almost automatic. You are now awake enough in the dream world that when the ego summons you with its wares you will immediately call on Me for translation, just as mt did after dreaming of the salesman. You wonder now about My use of the two terms: *mt* and *you*. This is also part of the discernment process. Mt is the ego self, a character, a figment of the imagination playing a role on the dream stage that allows her to be a channel for My purpose. Mt is not real. Her "reality" exists in the mind as a decision maker, the "you" who gets to choose each moment between your true Self or the false ego self. We are watching the mt character in her role in the world of form. In last night's dream, she followed the directions of the ego and willingly listened to its spiel. When you get tempted by the ego, remember Me and know that mt is only acting out a fantasy.

Mt is a manifestation of the split mind, a thoughtform having no substance. She is a projected dream character being used as a vehicle to bring the mind back to wholeness through her awakening to the truth that "she" is none other than the Christ Self, the One Son of God. This is true for every character. In this moment, you and I are above the battleground, the playing field of life, so you can watch how it unfolds without taking it seriously. You are joined with Me, and that is how we maintain our witnessing vantage point.

You can discern the difference between being joined with Me or with the ego that would keep you attached to the elements of the dream that do not serve your highest purpose. You will be provided with what is needed to sustain this earthly life, but you will know that it is not real, only a form that allows Me to bring you and all your many selves to full awakening. The three of you have come far in this realization. You call on Me whenever you are challenged by the ways of your ego. Each stress, discomfort, or judgment is a reason to call on Me. In fact, every thought that is not of kindness is a reason to call on Me. I am present now in your mind throughout a significant part of your day. This conjunction between us will continue to increase over time until we are united in the Now. The awakened state you see demonstrated by Byron Katie and Eckhart Tolle is to be your life, and it will be the life of all readers in their own designated time of readiness. You feel the perfection of that promise because a new certainty has filled your being. We rejoice at this new chapter in this new estate. Celebrate your Life in Me. We are One, and we will demonstrate our Oneness to all who can see.

Is there more, Holy Spirit? No, you can call your sister now. (I called Susan, and she said she is no longer comfortable with full-time male companionship. She is ready to live her own life. I asked the Holy Spirit about her.) Susan is in My hands and is ready to see this realization through My Vision. She knows Me and is learning to love her Self. My sustenance is all she needs. This is her last lifetime of suffering the absence of love. She is your Sister in Me and we are One. You must release the idea that you are superior or more advanced. Susan has also come a long way, and you both will be united with Me. Where you go, your brother goes with you. Take her as your partner and see her only as the reflection of your Self. You go joined because there is no hierarchy of illusions. Yes, your ego would make you believe that you are better, that you know more and should go first. But the last shall be first. Susan has fought the fight, and you will enter Heaven together. *Holy Spirit, please open my heart fully to that knowing.* I will.

Live from Me

You enter the Kingdom joined.

January 2, 2014

Holy Spirit, what is Your instruction this morning? We will be together as One. Yesterday you had a very important message from Me. I have told you that you and your sister will enter Heaven together. This came as a slight surprise and was difficult for your ego to hear because you, as the older sister, always thought of yourself as the first one, the leader, the wiser, so, of course, *you* would enter the Kingdom first. That is not true, and you understand why it is the deepest lesson so far. You saw that she must go with you as your Self. Susan is your dream construction, and as that, she is one with you in the mind. There are no real differences. In form, you are of the same blood, womb, and father—symbolic of the reality that you are the same Thought of God. Susan has been your projection screen for all you would like to disown in yourself. Now you see she is one with you. Less than a week ago, she saw "My face" appear twice in her dreams. She, too, has identified with Me, as Me.

Years ago, when you had a taste of the real world and believed you were on the doorstep of enlightenment, you had the realization that you cannot enter Heaven alone. Your most surprising thought in that moment was "I will not become enlightened without my sisters Meera and Jo." This is the joining of which *A Course in Miracles* speaks. It is the recognition that there is no hierarchy of illusions and that you are all together, one and the same Self. You enter the Kingdom joined.

Your friend Andy called yesterday. He loves the *Course* and was reading Lesson 155, so you took it as a message to read it too: *I will step back and let Him lead the way.* This is where you now live with Me. You have stepped back, as has your sister and Andy, to let Me lead you. In the Workbook lesson, I spoke of those who demonstrate this state of surrender to My Authority and how they let truth go before them. When you demonstrate the peace of living from Me and not from the ego, it will be recognized by those who know Me. Others will see you only as a projection of their ego thought system. They cannot yet use you as a model of a way to reach the light of their own souls.

Last night you walked your favorite beach to celebrate the birth of the New Year and the start of our next book. You found an unusual shell in the incoming wave and showed it to a man nearby named Emmanuel. He was from the Caribbean, and in the first minutes of your speaking, you both realized you share the knowing of Me as all there is. It was a gift to hear the story, identical to your own, of how he was guided by his Christ Self to leave his home and family and move to Maui three years before you did. You each live your lives for Me and from Me and felt the joy and peace of having the same understanding of who you are in God. It reminded you of the *Course* lesson: *Teachers of God recognize each other.* Yes, you were to have that thought reinforced and grounded. I am everywhere, in every one, which you both had the eyes to see.

Every brother is your Self. Every brother carries My face, the face of Christ. Everyone is you whether they have come to the realization that I am their only Self or not. Everyone you meet in mind or form is an extension of the Thought of God and a projection of your own thinking. See them all as a reflection of your truth in Me. Welcome each one back into your heart and know you are welcoming them to enter Heaven with you, joined as One.

Repeated Lifetimes

Life in a dream world is a hollow repetition
of meaningless cycles.

January 3, 2014

Holy Spirit, what is Your instruction today? We have come far. This was represented in your early morning dream—a dream of awakening. Although you had no body awareness, you felt suspended in a vaporous "knowing" of what was taking place around you. It appeared you were swinging on two copper tubes attached to a dark wall. Your life and safety depended on their reliable connection, but you noticed that one of the tubes had become detached. The copper had been drawn back to expose a coil that was expanding, but somehow you did not fall. You knew the tubes were very valuable, and the owner would be angry because the apparatus would be expensive and difficult to repair. This brought fear, and you could not imagine confronting him with your carelessness. When you woke up, you had the clarity that the situation was all happening in the mind of mt, a dream figure who does not exist. You were also aware that in the dream, mt had held great symbolism in her hands.

What do You say, Holy Spirit? As mt, you believe you are still attached to the coils of repeated lifetimes of births and deaths, like being attached to a wall with limited vision. In the dream, you could not see where you were. The blank black wall should have prevented you from swinging from the tubes, but you did not feel anything stopping you. With My help, you are able to witness everything that has blocked you for lifetimes of wanting to swing free. Until now, you did not have the tools to become released, to see what was waiting for you behind the wall of not knowing. Yes, you have asked to be in the state of "not knowing," and you are. It is from this place of trust that your dream is being revealed with its true meaning: the dreamer is all parts of the dream. Let us look at them more closely.

The wall is the mirror of the ego mind, a picture of man's mistaken beliefs about himself that leave him in darkness. Man thinks he knows what is right in front of him, yet he sees nothing because he is nothing, just as "you were swinging" but unaware of a body that was swinging. In the dream, you had no concept that you could go beyond the dark wall to a place of light and freedom. The hanging copper tubes represent your attachment to the elements of the earth and are what allow transmissions of communication in the world of form. The exposed coils inside the core of the tubing symbolize the uncovering you have done. You now see that the experience of your earth life is just one continuous spiral of the same unending story.

Life in a dream world is a hollow repetition of meaningless cycles. Unless they are seen for their falsity they can never set you free. You suffered no damage when the attachment to the wall of darkness was broken. Your only fear was the repercussion from the owner of the paraphernalia. Of course, you realize this is the symbol for your ego thought system. It would tell you that you are in supreme danger for cutting the cord to its womb of safety that protected you from God. The fear of God's punishment becomes your fear of the ego's retaliation for letting go of its hold on you, which would liberate you from the cycles of birth and death. The ego fears for its life. You, on the other hand, can wake up and feel the freedom of realizing it was all just a dream, that you are unharmed and have the means, through Me, to know the truth. This allows you to go beyond the wall of darkness into the light. There is no punishment. There is nothing to fear. You have worked steadily, year after year, to uncover the secret to true liberation—you are the dreamer of a dream of fear, which you created to keep from knowing your Self. You now know Me as your Self and trust that I will lead you on the journey to God. We have come far and you are at the final steps.

Yesterday was a milestone for your sister. She was able to break the cycle of attachment to a string of failed relationships, all substitutes for My true Love. All outward seeking is every reader's experience, lifetime after lifetime. The unending chain of partners gave Susan great heartache and sorrow, but she was finally able to see that her "own life" depended on the truth of her Beingness, her Self, her Life in Me. She has repeatedly called on Me for guidance. I have shown her that she needs no one other than her Self for satisfaction and comfort. This is a huge lesson and is hard won. She has worked diligently for her liberation and experienced it yesterday, saying no to the last male relationship that would bind her.

Yes, the Light has come. This is the Way of My Vision, which clearly shows you only what is real—the connection to Me as your Self and your Guide. Attachments to form are never real. When you see there is another way than a life of separation, you will no longer be up against an immovable wall of darkness. You will be free to decide with Me how to navigate the dream world until you are fully awake and ready to return Home. The chains of repeated birth and death have been broken, and freedom of Life in Me is now revealed. *Thank You, Holy Spirit, for this sense of liberation and the freedom You have given to the three of us and to Susan.*

The Only Knower

All things are My messages,
and I am the only One to interpret them.

January 4, 2014

Holy Spirit, please help me understand my attachment to this role as scribe. I will. As a vehicle for the Holy Spirit, you have been asked by Me to transcribe My words for a series of books to be shared with those who study *A Course in Miracles* and others who also want to wake up. You have surrendered faithfully to My direction. Today we look at your role in terms of its meaning to the form and personality of you, as mt, in the world. Mt has had many lifetimes as a scribe for Me and for her own purposes. You are aware of one lifetime where you sat with a crystal ball giving predictions to men who were eager to believe your soothsaying but then saw their lives fall into disrepair. At the end of that lifetime, you imagined destroying God and the universe as you killed yourself. Yes, I told you that you are very attached to the role of scribe, but you have now come to the point of telling Me, "Thy Will be Done." You are even willing to surrender this role, if necessary, to find complete peace within your Self. In the last week, you have had the experience of "knowing" you know nothing and that you are not the Knower. This has opened a door for you to look deeper into your past attachment to advising both those in positions of power or anyone seeking your counsel.

Through your recollection of a past life as a seer, you realized that to be an advisor is actually the ego's means of usurping the Power of God from the soul of the advisee. You would take from him the ability to access his own Inner Knowing, the only thing that can deliver his truth. When you channel the "word of God" to a person in a position of power, you, like the oracle of ancient times, become more powerful than that one. You must look at the role of advisor from above the battleground and witness how destructive it can be when it is not being delivered in perfect surrender to Me. To be an ego personality in the role of a channeler of divine wisdom, for someone who believes that you have the answers for his life, is to be a "killer" of the Christ Self in you both. This powerful role of "ego as advisor" must be released. You always share My words with Jo and Meera, and without the two of them, you would not have reached this point of awareness—to see everyone as yourself, all equal with Me, as One.

I repeat: to usurp another's power of knowing is to "kill the Christ" of him. The ego self can't know for another. You know nothing. I am the only Knower, and you surrender to that. You are Me. That is all. Any role performed on earth is inconsequential. It doesn't matter. The role of channeler, scribe, knower of answers, when performed through the ego, gives one the belief that their power is equal to God's and becomes a means for believing the ego's answers are right. To Not know is the only way Home. It is total relinquishment of everything to Me. You thought you knew the answers for men. Now you know that "men" are not real and that all knowing exists beyond human comprehension. You know nothing of the mind. So this is where we begin.

Relinquish all "knowing." I will direct your thoughts and actions. *Holy Spirit, I would give up this role of scribe if You asked. I admit that it has been a valued identity to which my ego personality is attached. I ask to be released into Your hands for whatever task You give Me, just to be with You.* You now realize that to be "the advisor" becomes more important than the One Who is advising. God is left out, and only a powerful ego self remains. Give all desire for knowing, to Me.

(Afternoon) *Holy Spirit, is there more You would say?* You have already had a number of messages from Me today. All things are My messages, and I am the only One to interpret them. You, in your incarnation as mt and scribe for these books, are only a receptacle, a vehicle for Me to put My words into the world for all who have the ears to hear. You were very touched, a few moments ago, when your sister Susan said that you and she, along with Jo and Meera, were all together with me in my lifetime on earth as Jesus. She also said that most people did not understand Jesus's message at the time and that most do not, or will not, understand the messages you are now transcribing. You were surprised that Susan gave you such specific information because it would not be her propensity to make that kind of declaration. Yes, we were all together, and that is what "attaches you" to Me in this lifetime. You and Susan were to come to a point of joining as one and the same. You each accept that I am the Doer. Together, we are "doing this" as an exercise, but the real effect is happening in the mind you share with all humanity.

Fear of Joy

Joy is the absence of suffering.

January 5, 2014

Holy Spirit, what is Your instruction? We will continue the work of the night. You were given help, at your request, to remove the veils that cover your joy. All your life you have felt the repression of joy and were suspicious of others who expressed unbounded bliss. You felt they were acting in ways that were false so you backed away from them in your mind. You could never understand your mother's expressions of joy because you believed she had suffered too much to really have that capacity. You were known by all to be too serious and were constantly asked by your husband to "lighten up." Inside, you could understand that something was missing, but you did not know how to access it. Your piano teacher once commented, "Your mother stole your joy." You lived with a mother who had suffered unimaginable loss at age nine with the death of the two caretakers she loved most, her mother and her grandmother. You believed that to be loved by God and to be fully accepted by your mother, you would need to suffer even more, a belief that was never fully conscious.

Later in your life, a friend who practiced shamanism told you she would perform a shamanic journey to help you find your joy. This is how loss is seen in the human condition, no matter what the form. You believe someone took it from you, usually a parent. You now see that the belief that you "do not deserve joy" began as a result of leaving the Joy of Heaven. That choice brought the notion of "God's wrath" into your mind. Yes, it is convoluted, and this is the condition of a world set up in the ego mind to be the opposite of Life in Heaven. Therefore, to feel joy is to call forth guilt and punishment and to live in suffering is to be "loved by God." *A Course in Miracles* makes this concept clear when it describes how pain, suffering, and sacrifice are thus equated with "happiness" in the world of form.

Last night you looked deeply with Me at your fear of joy. It required great willingness for you to take back the projection you had placed on a friend, who, in your opinion, was too exuberant. It appeared that her focus was only on the material world and thus not worthy of Divine acceptance. Yes, you were tapping into your deepest belief that God *wants you* to suffer for your transgression in leaving Him, which never happened, yet is the underpinning of your life in the physical realm. To feel joy was to lose the Love of God. It is that simple. Now you feel tears of recognition. You know Me as the expression of the Voice for God, and you do feel My Love. It became clear after pages of writing that you believed "suffering is the most direct route to God." For that reason, you had to dismiss the joy expressed by your friends, believing you would never reach the capacity for that same joyfulness. This is the belief that you would never reach Heaven, would never be acceptable to God, and would never feel the Presence of Love in your heart. We have now looked at your fear. It has been seen with Me and acknowledged by you. You have pleaded for My help and have received My Blessing.

My Constant Joy has always been the foundation of your Being, but your belief in punishment was so great that it overrode the power of your truth. Your resistance to those who expressed great joy was really your own projection onto them of your fear of joy. Judgment was how your ego kept you in the belief that suffering and the denial of joy would keep you safe. Without a belief that joy could ever be yours, you could not come to the full realization of your birthright: the Joy of God. You had to see that this was your choice before you could set the brother free to experience his life without your judgment. That set you free as well. Now you wonder if you will actually experience this shift. Yes, and we will celebrate the lifting of a veil that has kept you from your Self for lifetimes. Remember, to actually experience the Joy of God means the death of your ego.

Without being willing to witness the reflection of the beliefs projected onto your brother, and the willingness to take back those judgments, you would not be free. You have worked tenaciously throughout your life to find the truth of your being, and to release all that would hold you back. We are dealing with the deepest layers of the separation, and the Light is shining brightly to make the shadows of fear disappear. I am working with your many selves to remove all barriers to the knowing of My Joy, which is the Joy of every Being. You ask now the real meaning of Joy. It is the absence of suffering; it is the ability to be with "what is" in full acceptance and embrace. It is the knowing that I Am all that Is. There is no other. There is no fear. Only Love remains when you release the thought of suffering. This is what sets the mind free to come Home. Now let this assimilate.

You need not think that you must express the same kind of exuberance you see in others. Each has his own means of expression. For you, the experience of joy will be the feeling of connection with Me without barriers and fulfilling your purpose of scribing the books. You are free to enjoy your life fully with no mental anguish. *So, Holy Spirit, would You say that each one with You can handle and accomplish his chosen task, his life's purpose, with grace and ease?* Yes. You know this now. You do not resist your commitment to Me.

6

Threads of Attachment

The Presence of My Love in you
is the agent of healing.

January 6, 2014

(Day of Epiphany) *Holy Spirit, what is Your instruction?* You have just been asked to surrender all thought to Me, and this request has set your ego into fear. It is now bombarding you with thoughts of death, illness, and disaster. Notice how rapidly they arise after I tell you to wait for My guidance before every action and make no future plans. You want to attend your yoga class today and fear I will tell you not to go. That thought is of the ego. It would create fears that the pleasures in your life will be stolen by Me or that you will become sick and die. This is how the ego works. We watch its silly maneuvers from above. My will is not for you to suffer or to take away the enjoyment of your life on earth. You can go to your class, and you will hold Me in your mind as all there is.

You have been thinking about Ken Wapnick and wondering how things are going at the Foundation without him. His passing was peaceful and planned. Know that I am in charge of all that is happening for the *Foundation for Inner Peace* and the *Foundation for A Course in Miracles*. All who are connected with *ACIM* are part of this transition. It is a reorganization in form, planned from the very beginning. You will also feel its effects, but there is nothing for you to be concerned about. I have it handled and will give you your role in time.

This early morning, you dreamed of trying to break a nylon thread. As much as you intended to pull it apart, and no matter

19

how hard you tried, the thread would not break. This reflects the strength of connection you have to Ken and the founders of *A Course in Miracles.* You do feel this, and it brings tears of recognition. You will now be a holder of the torch for them in the mind. Your commitment to be a beacon is strong and will be guided by Me. There is nothing for you to do in form. Just Be with Me and hold to your love of the *Course* and its continuation. It is not about your future with our books; it is about My intention to bring these concepts to the world. You protest that you are too old, that someone younger needs to be in this role. Remember, there are many who are holding the light for the continuance of these ideas, and it is most important at this time for you to be willing to continue the work. Only that is necessary. The beacon shines its loving light, and the work will be carried forward into the next generation. You need not know more than that, but there is already a shift in your mind of which you are aware.

Hold all brothers with the Light of My Love, confident that nothing they do will be done in vain. You have joined them in their efforts, knowing that the work goes on. You are one with them and always have been. This brings you all together in the mind. The physical world has fallen away in this moment; form is meaningless. The intention to carry forward the teachings of the *Course* is what matters. Yes, that, too, is form, but it is an important focus for the mind of man. We are dealing with wholeness, unity, forgiveness, peace, and love, and our goal is to bring these concepts to the forefront. *Is this for the book?* Yes, and it is a message to all readers to hold everything in a mind-space of love. That is the way to see everything in your world.

Envision now a soft light embracing those who are reorganizing and planning how to carry forward after Ken's death. Your love and support are all that is needed. You do not know the power of intentional love to heal the world, but this message is a means for you to feel that love and send it off with My blessing. The Presence of My Love in you is the agent of healing. I will guide you in this practice. You are becoming more aware of the interconnectedness of all selves and all things and have felt a part of this transition with the founders of the *Course*. You are all united in the intention to awaken from the dream of separation. Shed the Light of Peace and Love to all your brothers. My Work, My Word, and My Love go forward into eternity.

Myriad Selves

When you give someone your full attention,
you are really giving it to Me.

January 7, 2014

Holy Spirit, what is Your instruction for today? We will review a particular dream from last night. You were standing in a room. On your right was a table, stacked high with pint-sized jars of pure water that had been sent from different parts of the environs. Three men were pouring what you thought was the water into a huge thermos, but what you saw looked like chai, the milk tea at Sai Baba's ashram in India that is served to thousands from all over the world. In your dream, you watched how the men carefully poured the sterile milk tea into the thermos, holding their fingers out so there would be no contamination. You were confused about how the water had become tea.

This is a powerful message to you and all the readers of this book: pay attention to everything you are offered every moment of your day. It is a gift to you from Me. Neglect nothing. Every event, every thought, every meeting holds an offering to be distilled by Me into a nectar for your soul. I transform every image to feed you My wisdom and instruction for the process of your awakening. All the offerings blend into the drink of love for those who are ready to imbibe. You are surprised to see how I now use your experience at the ashram to give My message of the morning. Everything is used; do not ignore any experience that comes your way. You would like to escape certain time-consuming activities or not pay attention to another's comments or stories because you think you have better things to do. Stop;

wait; listen. I have set them before you to deliver an instruction. Take the time to surrender in that moment to Me. Listen and know that I am behind every encounter. Let the movie run to the end with your calm and patient attention. Yes, it requires patience in loving service to fulfill My purpose, which you are willing to do.

These books are a compilation of your many experiences in the world of form. I have transformed those details into an offering to be used by the thousands to come to a better understanding of the Self. We are all the One Son, but in the illusion, it appears that man is separated into many forms and appearances. You are now taking in the contributions of all the iterations of the Sonship. Each one you meet represents one of the aspects, or facets, of the whole. When you give someone your full attention, you are really giving it to your Self, Me. It is the Self fully listening to its Self. Each of you then adds your unique ingredient to the one blend, which can feed nations in the mind.

You, mt, in your emptiness, are ready to be filled by all the offerings of those you meet from around the world, but first, you must remain empty of your ego's demands to have life "your way"—keeping space and time to your little self. Many readers have experiences, not unlike mt's, while meeting the brothers in form, in the media, or in their thoughts. Each encounter activates a response from your ego, a desire to judge or discount the other in some way so the ego can remain in charge and superior. This is what we notice together now, joined above the battleground. Ask to be lifted above your reactions so you can receive the brothers openly and without judgment, remembering they are all reflections of your Self. Then, the container of your open heart will be ready to receive the pure waters of a brother's essence and the gift he has to offer for your own completion. With his offering, you are preparing to make ready for the "tea," which I will then serve back to you, transformed and purified, to be received as My blessing. Now that you, mt, have opened to Me as a channel, I can pour forth the distillation of all your experiences.

> (I do feel I have settled into my role with the books now. There is a gentle joy of embracing, receiving, and sharing them. There is peace and appreciation, without feeling special, just an acceptance of "it is what it is." It seems my capacity to receive all that comes from the Holy Spirit has increased. As I sat in the hot tub tonight with six other people, it was like sharing a big cup of tea together.)

The Invisible Engineer

I am the Power and Presence that knows the way Home.

January 8, 2014

Holy Spirit, what is Your instruction? You were given a powerful dream just before you woke up. I placed a message in it, which we deciphered, and then you went to the computer. Now we will encapsulate that dream experience. You found yourself on a mountain with a group of unfamiliar people who would be running a race at 1:00 p.m. after eating a special lunch and taking a shower. You would have had to pay $80 for the lunch, but you ate your own instead. Then you became concerned that the super-food might have allowed you to run the three miles, but you also knew that your legs would not carry you that far. All of a sudden, you were inside the mountain looking out a window, peering down to a great hall below. There you saw a long black train with endless compartments being washed by invisible cleaners. You felt a comfort in looking at the careful cleansing, seeing the suds coming out of the train's windows and doors. You were standing on a narrow marble ledge and knew you would be jumping down to the successive ledges below—each about four feet wide—to reach the ground. You had managed the first one but had some fear about the next jump.

What is Your interpretation? In a nutshell, the "you" on the mountaintop, awaiting a race that made no logical sense, is you as mt living in the world of form. Nothing here makes any sense, and you now feel yourself an outsider to the world you inhabit. In the night dream, you are uncertain which rules to follow to understand the sense of "rightness" that you feel internally. You

27

are unsure of the expectations from your environment. You do pay attention to what you know is true for you by not engaging in a meaningless competition. Then you find yourself in a great hall that reaches from the top of the mountain to the base. This represents the mind, which is massive and holds yet hidden information. You show up and are willing to observe what is below. You take the leaps of faith that will lead you to the Ground of Knowing.

At first, the image of the train filled you with comfort because it was being so well cared for, but when I told you the train is Me, you experienced fear. Because you couldn't imagine why I would take the form of a train, the ego mind immediately associated it with Holocaust trains heading for the concentration camps. You asked for clarity and I told you that the train is My vehicle to bring you Home. It is powerful and safe. You will be carried to your destination with certainty that it is all in My hands; nothing can derail the plan. The ego then reminded you that three trains were stuck in subzero weather for hours yesterday, near Chicago. All these fears show you how the world of form distorts the truth, turning every positive into a negative. My Train will reach the Station.

You have realized that the train also represents your deepest desire to share your journey of hearing My Voice with the world. We are joined, and you are being shown the vehicle for that distribution. The train, in its multiple, unending compartments, will carry all the many selves to their destination through the vehicle of the books, which are being transported to the world of form. In the dream, the train has no visible engineer or cleaners. This is an expression of the unseen realm of the mind where all of this is really taking place.

I am the Power and the Presence, the invisible Engineer Who knows the way and Who will lead you all at your point of readiness to your true Home in God. Overlook fear and move forward to put the books into the world. You feel love for Me and for this mission we share. There is joy in the acknowledgment that your purpose is unfolding. It is being fulfilled as we write because the mind receives these messages and feels its liberation. There is nothing more to say other than to ask each reader to trust that every vehicle is being provided as a tool for his awakening. Ask Me the meaning of anything that arouses a question in your mind. I will show you its significance, and that will take you the next step. You shall all board My Train Home.

Surrender

We all inhabit the same room, the same heart,
and together we compose the One Son of God.

January 9, 2014

Holy Spirit, what is Your instruction this evening? We did not write this morning as you were in the midst of experiencing a revelation that has taken you deep. You dreamed of a woman who did not recognize the work you had done, nor could you see her as having any knowledge. You judged her severely for not seeing your capabilities and were unwilling to give her a chance to demonstrate hers. Then an opening took place where you had a conversation. It turned out that you both had been dealing with the same specialty, one which today is rarely mentioned: working with survivors of satanic ritual abuse. You discovered that she was very skilled in this field and had up-to-date experience as a therapist. You then were able to embrace her as an equal.

When you woke up, you associated this dream with an experience you had in Sai Baba's ashram in 1991. It was the most profound experience of your life, up to that point, because you clearly saw the Hand of the Divine in it. At the same time in your career as a clinical social worker, many clients were showing up in your practice who had been ritually abused and were experiencing severe states of dissociation and multiple personalities. You felt privileged to do this difficult work, grateful you were able to help them access the light of their being as they became acquainted with the many still-held wounded "personality states" within their unconscious. By the time you visited Sai Baba, you had a deep desire for his help in how to proceed with your clinical practice.

At the ashram, you were fortunate to stay in a single room, but after ten days you had to give it up. You were then assigned to a space on the floor of a huge shed with hundreds of cots. As you prepared to gather up your few belongings, a man appeared at your door with a notice to go to yet another room. The rules would not allow you to sleep in anything but the shed, so you asked the office personnel what to do. They told you to go to the new room, although it was already occupied by an American woman, her child, and a French woman. You knew there were a handful of Americans in the ashram among the thousands of Indians and people from all over the world. When you knocked on the assigned door, a woman answered in English and told you the room was full and that she "refused" you. Exhausted, you returned to the office. You had been sick for several days with dysentery. The office told you to return and to tell the woman she couldn't refuse you. You returned and knocked. She opened the door, and you both looked deeply into each other's eyes. Finally, she said, "I get the message you should come in." She then gave you a small space on the floor of the tiny room.

> (The woman and I sat on the floor, and she began to talk. Almost immediately she said that she had been in the ashram for three weeks and had found no one with whom she could discuss her past ritual abuse. I was overcome with emotion, knowing I was led to her room by unseen forces to be the exact help she was seeking. In tears, I told her I was a therapist for ritual abuse and that I would help her any way I could. We set a time to begin our therapy the following morning, but when the time came I was suddenly overcome with laryngitis. She, at the same moment, told me she was getting

the message we were *not* to do therapy. Instead, we were to enjoy the companionship of sharing a room together. We were to just Be. It was one of the greatest miracles and blessings in my life to be with her for the next five days.)

Holy Spirit, is this what You wanted? Yes, it is our story, and Baba is My instrument, an Instrument of God, bringing you the message that we are all one. No one knows any more than another. You are all engaged in surrendering to the Way of God and to the release of all association with the ego thought system, represented in this story as satanic abuse. Stories and characters are all the same—while one is evil, the other holds superior knowledge. The ego would take charge of every relationship to make one the victim and the other the savior. You see this played out everywhere you look. At the ashram, in a weakened condition, and with the desire to open to the spiritual blessings of being in that holy place, you were in a state of surrender. You followed the directions you were given, and they led to a deep realization that all personalities, whether in mind or form, are the same. They all belong to you.

You are coming to see that each person in your imagination or in your life is really just a reflection of you. You mirror each other, and you meet to learn this very lesson. The character in your dream last night symbolized you entering the room of the ritually abused woman, years ago at the ashram. Your dream character told you she knew all about ritual abuse and could give you the most up-to-date information. At that moment, you dropped all judgment and welcomed her as a sister. We all inhabit the same room, the same heart, and together we compose the One Son of God. The ritual abuse work was a way to see that all the multiple personalities of your many clients are no different from all your many selves, those you encounter by the dozens every day. You are learning to welcome them with openness and kindness and to consult Me whenever you feel a twinge of judgment. We are on the Homestretch now, joining with all brothers as One.

10

Universe of Light

All parts of the universe are of the Essence and Love of God, out pictured in diverse forms and distant worlds.

January 10, 2014

Holy Spirit, what is Your instruction this morning? You have been looking at the face of Venus on your iPad, an image that appears not unlike the earth. You have also seen a program showing the possibilities of life on a planet like yours, light-years away. What is the meaning of seeing those images of your distant neighbors? When you moved into your condo of 440 units, ten years ago, you had no desire to meet your neighbors. You wished to remain isolated and felt yourself special and separate. Over the years, you have realized they are representations of your many selves, and you have welcomed them with generosity and warmth. When you hold your iPad's Star Walk app over your balcony you bring the universe closer into view. It is a reflection of bringing Me closer into view.

As we have become more acquainted, you have felt more inclusive of everyone in your world. You think of the man you believed was homeless who has greeted you often under the Banyan Tree, telling you how seeing you would bless his day. Yesterday, when you greeted him, he said it was the fifth anniversary of his sobriety and that he felt the blessing of your presence. A genuine warmth and love had been expressed under My auspices. You actually felt that love all day long as you worked at the gallery while many of the artists appeared for a variety of needs. Rather than being annoyed at the frequent distractions, you welcomed each one as a part of the Self. Your joy was evident, and the day unfolded with an unusual ease in the face of all the demands for your attention. The planets have been "witnessed" as representations of your own projected self, and you are close to being ready to welcome any of their inhabitants as neighbors, friends, or other reflections of that self. It all may sound far-fetched, but this is how the return Home looks and feels.

The universe is now "collapsing," being reined in so that you can view it with new understanding, with My meaning. I interpret everything you see as a reflection of the Self you truly are. All parts of the universe are of the Essence and Love of God, out pictured in diverse forms and distant worlds. Clearly, the far reaches of the universe are now under deep scrutiny. You have been inspecting the elements of your internal universe, which is a microcosm of that greater macrocosm. You had to look at all the aspects of your psychological being to uncover the beliefs that are untrue. Yes, viewing the planets and solar system is an out picturing of taking a careful look at the inner system that binds you to repeated lifetimes of fear and darkness. The ego thought system would keep you blind to the Light of your Being, your only true nature and the essence from which the universe was created. Love is as God is as Light is. The Universe of Light exists in you, and this is what we have been uncovering, layer after layer, for many years, by removing all belief in separation—a belief that has been projected onto your neighbors and your brothers.

As long as you believe the brother's essence is any different from your own, you will see him through the eyes of fear. No matter what his race or what role he plays in the world, you have learned that any judgment your ego projects onto him keeps you separate and verifies you are not One in the Love of God. To pay attention to every speck of an unforgiving thought, as you look upon a brother, is the way to navigate your inner world and bring the thought to Me. Together, we can turn around the belief that one is superior while the other is inferior. In My Light, you are able to take back the fearful projections that would continue the experience of separation for eternity. As they disappear—one after the other, day after day, year after year—you begin to feel a lightness in your own being. Your brothers can now approach because you welcome them as your Self. They are being drawn to the Light of My Presence within you, which shines without impediment. That Light ignites your brother's light so that he, too, may feel his own brilliance and seek for his truth.

Signs of the awakening are now being seen throughout humanity. Although many believe this world is unique in the cosmos, others are more open to the idea that they are not alone, that "neighbors" do exist. This realization is a mirror for the Son of God to learn that he is not alone; every brother, every speck of dust he sees has its origin in a Thought of God and is a reflection of an aspect of himself. The collapse or disappearance of the universe is not about form; it is realizing that we are all sharing the same Mind. You all can hear My Voice as the One Self, which each and everyone reading this book shares with Me. *Holy Spirit, is this all?* Yes. Go about your day. I am there each moment. Remember that every brother is a reflection of your ego thought system but needs to be seen as your Self, not in form but as part of the One Mind. Together, we remember our Essence as One with God.

Note from Margie:

Tonight I received a long message from Jo and realized it was about so much more than her beloved eleven-year-old cat. The Holy Spirit said to include it. He refers to its significance in later messages.

Email from Jo: Today, Chi was diagnosed with a cancerous tumor of the salivary glands. I became overwrought, really sad at the idea his death could be imminent, so I asked the Holy Spirit to help me understand and release this strong attachment. I'm including our conversation. He said: "Chi represents the purest, most innocent part of yourself. You mourn what you believe would be the loss of that innocence in you both. Have no fear, these are soul qualities that can never die. You have misidentified yourself and Chi, seeing the limits instead of the truth of beingness. You must see beyond the body, and above, with Me, to really feel and know what you truly are: *Spirit.* The familiar, soft, body-form of a pet cannot be of truth or of God because it withers and dies. Your essence is never-changing, nor is Chi's, which feels to you like pure love and tenderness and deeply touches your heart. Release his body and yours in your mind. It no longer serves in the way it has been; it must go without any thought of loss. To release Chi is to release your own false life on earth and all attachment to it."

Holy Spirit, why do I cry so hard? "You cry for your little self that seems to be slipping away; you cry as there is no hope of saving this body or world. That fact is finally hitting you. The depth of your belief in separation is being felt for the first time, which must happen so it can finally be released. The tumor in Chi's mouth is still attached, eating away the body, but even a tumor is part of the gift. Chi became your heaven on earth, and the thought of his death brings back the thought that 'heaven is lost and you can't ever get it back.' The mistake is believing that heaven is easily replaced with the things of this world. Then you settle for second best and live out your life as a punishment. This is the trick of substitutions and distractions, which can never be enough. Let go of what you made up to save you. It can't because when it dies, you'll be left with nothing, no hope of returning Home. You do know what to do: give Me every body and image and thought and fear and belief and attachment. Let it all go, and you'll rejoice that nothing ever happened to keep us separate."

Holy Spirit, I do see the depth of my own attachments to this life as a self. "When you anticipate loss, you fear having nothing left to fall back on, to enjoy. You think you'll be all alone when your substitutions leave. Fear is the root of all the anxieties and worries that have plagued you for lifetimes; you were always anticipating the worst, being left with no defense. Yes, all substitutions are a defense against the truth. Without them, the ego is 100 percent fear, and Spirit feels out of reach. You must see what the belief in separation has wrought. Release everything to Me before you see any more signs of 'death.' There is no death. Let it go now. Bring Me the images, the bodies, the thoughts of loss so I can show you what is nothing and what is Everything. Release every last one and Be Free." *Thank You, Holy Spirit. I see that only my little self can suffer. In this moment, I am no longer sad, and I feel Your gifts.*

11

Disable the Ego

The ego is a fantasy that accompanies you in this life;
it believes it is you.

January 11, 2014

Holy Spirit, what is Your guidance this morning? You see with more clarity that you and I are one and the same. There is no other. We are all there is. You had a realization of this while contemplating Jo's experience around the impending death of her cat. Jo, through My help, realizes that "she and Chi" have the same essence. To really understand this concept, you had to imagine the process of releasing the body to the fire. In your mind, you saw Chi placed on the cremation platform. The fires blazed around the body, causing great heat and light, and consumed the insignificant form. The brilliance filled the screen of your mind, and all that remained was the I AM. There was great reassurance in knowing that it would be the same for any body or imagined form with no real substance; like ether, they disappear in a flash. You have wished all could witness death as the Indians do. They easily release the body to the flames or the vultures because they know the spirit never dies and they will reincarnate. Death is covered up in your society, so, for most, it remains a mystery that leaves confusion about its deepest meaning.

This early morning, you had an important dream. You were with your own brother and others, in a large field at dusk, collecting tall twigs and sticks. No one had any idea what the sticks were for, but each person sat quietly in front of a carefully prepared bundle. Nothing was happening other than the silence of waiting. After you woke up, you realized the sticks were for a fire, but not until now, as we write, do you realize that they all represented funeral pyres for each bundle-maker's ego thought system. Everyone in this dream world is waiting for the time of readiness to burn up his ego. You are all preparing for the moment of the conflagration of your body, personality, and world. To picture yourself on that burning pile is an exercise that can serve every reader of this book. Recognize that the body is nothing and must be consumed in the flame of the Holy Spirit, the Flame that burns away what is not real.

Mt took the time to imagine herself on a funeral pyre, burning away the body she now sees as aging and losing its former appeal. The ego then appeased her with how she interacts with people through the attraction of her personality, saying that many are drawn to her engaging ways. Yes, mt knows she has identified with that personality as valuable and superior. To lose it would be "a tragedy." You, as mt, have to see your attachment to the way you relate to people in the world. It is not your ego charm that draws people to you; it is the emanation of My Light within, which attracts. You know this on one level, but now you are ready to release all that is false: the self—the personality that has believed in its mt specialness.

You want nothing but Me as your Inner Being now and do not care to manifest as a special character. You have come to know Me as your Self. This has been a long process of releasing your projections of judgment on all the many selves, all the characters you encounter daily, and those throughout your past. As the projections go, so does the sense of exclusiveness. Seeing everyone in a state of wrongness was only to preserve your desired "rightness." Now you know Me and call on Me constantly to inform your decisions and interactions. I have become the central focus of your life, more important than your mt personality, which is slowly fading into the background. You have also given up your main external focus—selling your art under the Banyan Tree. It was a very special place and was an opportunity for mt to get lots of recognition from fellow artists and many tourists. You are with Me in the new space we have created. This is why you are able to take the next step toward the dissolution of your ego thought system.

In another dream last night, you were standing next to a huge brass wheel-like ring, which was sitting in a large basin of water. The wheel began to turn a post that had a huge metal picture frame attached to it. This odd form represents a projector for the movie screen of your life. It was antiquated, cumbersome, and nonfunctional, and as you noticed more closely, it had been broken. Tiny slivers of glass covered the floor near the empty frame; the shards could never be reassembled. This is a depiction of your disabled ego thought system. You can see its uselessness. Its oppressive weight and shape are just images in your mind of an operation that no longer serves. You can dismiss it and let it go forever.

All the pictures that have appeared on the screen of mt's life have shattered. They are meaningless. The frame is empty and will be filled only by Me because I am the Self that fills the screen of your mind. You will operate from Me, as Me. The mt self is gone as your "reality." I am your only reality and your only Voice. Because you have come to Me, the heart of your life, you can accept what I now tell you. Mt will still be a vehicle for My use in the dream world, but you know mt is not who you are. The "you" I refer to is the decision maker, the witness of the whole dream, the one who now chooses Me as the only Operator of your life, your thoughts, and your destiny. Yes, you are still aware of ego thoughts arising, and they will continue. When you refer them to Me they will immediately be dissolved. We operate as One, which has been the truth of our Essence from the very beginning. This is enough for now.

Holy Spirit, how can this really be understandable to me or the readers since it takes an ego to type these words, the same ego that also questions their truth? Yes, the ego still exists for you to operate in the dream, but it is not the core of your Being. You recognize Me as all that is real, true, enduring, constant, steady. I am always present, always loving, always placing you in the perfect space and time, and giving you dreams to help clarify the messages. I am the one behind this life in form—what you know as your ego thought system. It is not real. The ego is a fantasy, a mirage that accompanies you and believes it is you. But as the decision maker, you now know the ego is not your reality and that it is Me. This is established in the Mind. You are getting acquainted with the truth of My message and will be assimilating it over time—years, in fact. Accept that the ego thought system is dismantled, over. Although you live in an ego dream world, see it now through My Vision. This is all you need to do.

Email from Jo: I noticed that my thoughts about Chi were still pretty peaceful, but then I read your message. I see I can go even further. You saw the images of the burning, the pyre, the release of the body, and I had not yet seen that in my mind. I had imagined finding a dead cat body on the floor or the vet putting him to sleep. Now I will sit with the practice of "seeing" my body, as well as Chi's, in the fire, being consumed into nothingness. The flame is Love, and the burning is to reveal the truth beyond any idea of form. Let the ashes fly.

12

One or the Other

Special relationships are the source for the deepest work
of uncovering the ego patterns in your life.

January 12, 2014

Holy Spirit, what is Your instruction today? You are experiencing an
ego rebellion after My statement to you yesterday that its obsolete
thought system has disintegrated. Yes, *dis-integrated* is the word I
want because that is what is happening to your ego and what is
setting you free. Its dis-integration means that it is no longer
integrated into your mind as your self. Now you see clearly what
the purpose of our work has been: to loosen the hold of the ego as
ruler of your mind. All the thoughts in your head have been
assembled by the ego over lifetimes. For an "ego personality" to
work, the collective mind had to jibe with a system that sees the
world as the opposite of God. When His Thoughts are allowed to
enter your mind, they topple the ego thought system.

The ego must believe that it is in control and rules your life. It
is the thing that makes your perception, that has you view the
world according to its principle of win or lose, one or the other. Its
system is based on separation and division, while the Thought of
God is all inclusive. It is only about Oneness, Wholeness, and
Innocence. The two "systems" cannot coexist. Only one will get
you to Heaven, to completion, and reunion with God, and that
way is to disentangle yourself from the dream by looking at the
world through My Vision. Only by seeing it through the lens of
Wholeness, will the ego personality begin to collapse. All its
structures will be recognized as counterproductive to finding the
Way of the Return to God.

For most, the release of the ego is a slow, laborious process because its hold on the mind is extremely tenacious. The ego has been honed in the human collective mind for eons. Now is the time, in this endless chain of birth and death, that you are ready to see it all with new eyes, to stand above the world of battle and look impartially at the actions of your life. Watch the ego character you play in the world. See how she interacts with the projected aspects of the ego thought system, especially those with whom she has special relationships. They are the source for the deepest work of uncovering the ego patterns in one's life. The three of you have used this opportunity of working together with Me over the past decade to come to Self-realization by discovering the depth of those patterns. Together, we have uncovered layers of projections you've placed on your brothers and on your selves—layers that have existed in the unconscious for lifetimes. You each realized that all these patterns, which distanced you from your brother, were, in fact, the ego's tool to keep you distant from Me. The ego's only and ultimate purpose is to prevent you from knowing that the truth of your Being lies in your Identity as Me, the Self, the One Son of God.

The discovery and acceptance of your equality with your brother, and his with you, are the hardest lessons to learn because the ego's motto of one or the other is so ingrained. It will fight to your dying day to make you believe you are better or worse than your brother. This is the basis for all conflict, which manifests as wars between tribes and nations and among political parties all over the world. All conflict is designed to remind you that separation is the name of the game. In the beginning, the ego presented itself as a "protective device" to keep you from the imagined wrath of God for leaving the Garden. Of course, all of this is symbolic. The dynamic of the dream of separation is beyond the human brain's comprehension, but you do know that without the belief in separation the ego would not exist.

Through hearing My Voice and feeling My Presence guiding you in all your encounters, perceptions, pain, and confusion, you have come to trust that I am the Core of your Being. Nothing other than your relationship with Me has any real meaning. You three have been able to encourage and reinforce each other on this path to knowing your unity with Me. You have come together in My Name and feel My guidance in every aspect of your lives. The ego has not been able to maintain a firm hold because you have learned to call on Me whenever discomfort, mistrust, or judgment arises. You encourage each other to ask Me for help whenever you notice the ego trying to influence the other to become stuck in its interpretations. Yes, the ego is still present in your lives but you now know you are One with Me, and this is where the ego has in fact, been disabled. It can no longer be ruler and operator when you know I am in charge of everything. You have witnessed the perfection of your own life and the lives of each other. Your joining has been invaluable and has brought you to a fuller realization of Me. Yes, there is further to go, but now you go with a Partner who is only Love and Who will be your constant Guide and Companion. Embrace how far you have come to know Me as your Self. We will continue unto the end of the earth together. Now go about your day and remember Me in all you do. *Thank You, Holy Spirit, for this beautiful message, and for repeating it over and over in many different ways so this small mind can open to the truth that You reveal.*

(After writing down the message from the Holy Spirit, I went out to sit with Him on the rocks. On the way, I watched dolphins close to shore and whales in the distance. Sitting with my coffee and the gentle waves lapping my toes, I looked at the beauty of the scene and had a moment of seeing the perfection of everything: the miracle of the formation of a human fetus, the organization of all the cells of our body, the order of all the solar systems in the universe, and the dream that unfolds every day in what we believe is our life.

I then recalled a beautiful quote from Henry Kapono Ka'aihue: "There is no place that I'd rather be than home in these islands in the middle of the sea." I then stood to survey the horizon and the sky. When I saw the whales, I thought of my great-grandfather Lewis, who was here in 1827, and the fear he must have faced, at only twenty-one years of age, to be on a whaling ship in the middle of the sea. At that moment, the Holy Spirit clearly said, "You were Lewis." I asked if this were true, and He said yes. In that moment, it seemed like all the unanswered questions of my life came together. My ex-husband Tom, in his study of Lewis's journals, appeared to love Lewis more than me. Now I understood my connection to Tom from a whole new perspective. I sobbed with this realization and spoke again with the Holy Spirit. His morning message was of the disintegration of the ego thought system, and here I was experiencing a deep new level of integration.)

What do You say? This is a completion for you, and it now makes sense: you and Lewis are one in the dream. This is the truth, and you feel it. It is "in your genes" and is "yourself" in this life, the one who longs to know and is willing to surrender, the one with a pure heart. Take it in fully. This is all you need to know now. *Holy Spirit, that is so peaceful. I feel one with my dream self. I want to thank Tom. Do I tell him?* No, he must come to this realization on his own. His soul is joined with you/Lewis.

I see this place, Maui, with new eyes. I have become whole. Yes, you have surrendered your life to Me. *I imagine all the fear that*

Lewis had to release. It is mine. We are one. I wonder why I didn't ever suspect that I was his reincarnation. And, You did mention that before, but it didn't register. You are all one, and this is the first step to the experience of that oneness. You have now integrated the other/great-grandfather as yourself. To feel the power of the integration of your past identities with your present dream life reinforces the awakening process now taking place. Feel your unity with all that is. In the mind, all beings of past, present, and future are integrating into the One Son. It is a great gift to know this.

> (I continued to sit in silence with the Holy Spirit. I came to know that Tom, Lewis, and I are one; that in our deepest nature we are all the same. We have each carried the same goodness, the same honoring of the Divine, the same desire to be kind, and the same loyalty. We even shared the spirit of adventure. Tom must have loved what he believed about the essence of Lewis in me, and I loved the Lewis essence in him.)

Holy Spirit, how are we all one? It is I, the Self you recognize as "you/Lewis/Tom." It is the Christ Self, known and seen in the purity and clarity of intention, in the search for God; it is seen in the surrender to what is. It is the nature of Jesus that you each are. *You, Holy Spirit, as Jesus, are the common denominator; You are what we love in each other.* I have told you we were together in that lifetime, and you longed to return to Me, the only One you seek. Just as Tom sought to "know" Lewis, he seeks to know his Self. He seeks Me, he sought Me in you, and you sought Me in him. *(tears)* This is the mystery resolved in form. You had to know My Voice to accept this truth.

Sit with Me and know Me as the Self you love—the Tom Self, the Lewis Self, the Jesus Self. We are all the Christ Self. *Holy Spirit, did I have to be with Jesus to know this?* No, you could know Me as the heart of your brother. *Did I know You when I was Lewis?* Yes, you knew Me in the waves and the storms at sea. You called on Me to calm your fears and trusted I would bring you home safely. You knew Me deep inside *as* Jesus, and that memory has lingered into this lifetime. I am your true Home. You know Me now and always have.

13

Basis of Reincarnation

The opportunity for man to return to the planet, in a new body, feels like his salvation.

January 13, 2014

Holy Spirit, what is Your instruction today? I gave you an important dream just before you awoke this morning. You were in a class where you had to translate important information through your old camera. After some time, without getting any results, you realized that your camera's computer must be out of date. You decided to buy a new camera and have someone help you, but you felt very lost and confused, believing there was no way you could approach the teacher or your classmates for their assistance. It was a dream of failure and hopelessness, except for the glimmer of owning "another device" that could save you.

This is the dilemma of every human being at the end of another sojourn on the planet. He is asked to review his life by his inner teacher and to make sense of it, but instead consults his ego. It will be sure to tell him that he did not live his life correctly, if not, indeed, failed. The ego would say there is a possibility he could succeed if he has a new device and is born into a new life in the world of form. At that moment, a new brain and new body, in yet another environment, seems very appealing. The ego mind is desperate to have another chance to "do it right." The opportunity for man to return to the planet feels like his salvation. He'll do anything because he is desperate to make this "new" body pass the test of worthiness. Yes, the body is a product of the mind alone. It is not real and never has been, but in man's ego mind, it is fully real and must prove to man that his sojourn outside the Kingdom as an individual was worth his while. He will agree and sign on the dotted line, which will take him into the next dream of a life in form. It is so clear to you now that the "life" one signs up for is like the dream you just had this morning. The suffering that comes from believing you have "done it wrong" is so severe that you are eager to take a leap into a new "device," with only the simple thought, "The old one isn't working and I need another chance to get it right."

The Thought of God was never part of your ego mind because you lived in terror of never finding a way out of your imagined errors. You have known this state in many night dreams throughout your life, like missing a class so you could not pass the test. Everyone unconsciously believes that his life is a test of endurance to remain hidden from God. By maintaining "a special ego personality," man believed he had outsmarted God. When his time is up on earth, and there is no longer a chance for him to "pass the test"—believing his life has had sufficient meaning and value—then he will do anything to try again with new equipment. He will listen to the most convincing salesman, and the ego is always right there with the solution. The ego will allow you to continue "your life" by buying into a new venue, a more appealing setting or family than the one from which you came. It is easy in your desperation of fast approaching death to say to the ego, "Yes, I will take your hand and follow your instruction." It offers the incentive to win the next round and sends you off to a new setup with new parents in a new town. This is the basis of "reincarnation."

In your case, mt, you were born to a father in this lifetime who was your grandson in your last life. You came in connected to the family of your "origin." As a child, you visited Lewis's house, where your grandmother lived. You listened to his conch shells and looked at his scrimshaw carvings on a whale's tooth. Neither your father nor your grandmother spoke of Lewis. Growing up, you had no interest in him or his life until you and

Tom were planning your first trip to Hawaii in 2001. Tom had taken a great interest in Lewis's whaling log that you had in your possession. You had never paid any attention to it, but suddenly Tom became almost obsessed with Lewis and his life as a whaler. He delved deeply into all the elements of Lewis's life he could find and constructed a website with transcriptions of both your log and the one your sister had. Later, when you knew you would be moving to Maui, you became more interested in Tom's research because the logs described Lewis's landing in Lahaina, a place where you now work.

Before you moved, you often felt that Lewis was a presence at your breakfast table when Tom eagerly described each morning what he had learned about Lewis the day before. It clearly seemed that Lewis was more real and loved by Tom than by you. And you were pleased to see how much enjoyment Tom had in this pursuit. When you saw the photo of Lewis that Tom found a few years ago, you were deeply touched by the depth and kindness in his face. It was similar to the way you see both Tom and your father. You have known Tom in the depths of his being as one and the same with you. In your core, you knew you were both deeply connected with God, both intent on serving humanity. When I told you that you were Lewis, it all made sense—your resonance with him, your deep love of Tom, and his love for you and Lewis.

You do see that Lewis and mt are merely dream characters repeating lifetimes to "get it right." You realize this one is the completion for "Lewis the whaler." Yes, he was a deeply Christian man who surrendered to God throughout his life. You bring "him" the next and last step to the end of the chain of birth and death because you are awakening from the dream of unending lifetimes. You now allow yourself, and yourself as Lewis, to see the folly of cycle after cycle even when it appears that one returns to a former family and enters loving arms. That is not enough. The only arms that will truly welcome you and give you true Love and Peace, are Mine—Arms that embrace you in the Thought of God.

The desire to join is the greatest power on earth. It is really the desire to unite with your Christ Self, your Essence, your Being. The dream is over. No more returns are necessary except to Me. Remember, I am the solution to every imagined problem. I will guide you to your true Home. *Thank You for this explanation, Holy Spirit. There is much to take in. Is this all, for now?* Yes, be with these words over the coming days. We are moving quickly. You feel like you are on a roller coaster and do not know when you'll catch your breath. *Holy Spirit, I get it. I am Lewis; I am Tom; we are You. I am You and no other.* Yes.

14

Your Internal Master

You must fire all the "holders of wisdom"
who are not the true Self.

January 14, 2014

Holy Spirit, what is Your instruction this morning? You have been given a multitude of symbols in this dream life. Yesterday, you met with a new friend who feels My guidance yet is unaware that I am the One behind all she does, and that I lead the way. She mirrored what you had always desired to experience on the spiritual journey: a knowing of your Self, through whichever form would offer that to you. She appeared to have achieved that kind of closeness and was the picture of the devotion you imagined "necessary" to reach the goal of enlightenment. You both felt a deep connection with Sathya Sai Baba, but she was a pure devotee who received his messages and had her altar blessed with his *vibhutti*—just what you longed for. She knew that she was his beloved. You could not imagine what that would feel like, but you had always wanted it. This was never your experience with spiritual teachers. You remained an "outsider" even when they said you were "special" or gave you an important role in the organization. You were not able to access the love in your heart for them or truly feel their love for you. This has been a major dilemma and disappointment in your life. To be the favored of the guru had been your goal, and you approached that with your last teacher, a Sufi master who placed you as leader of one of his satellite groups. Although you believed he would do the job of opening your heart and enlightening you at the point of your death, you never really felt your heart open to him.

You realize now that "the guru" was a distraction, no matter how magical or wonderful his miracles could be. You can laugh at how you projected all the power, majesty, and love within your own heart and soul onto the external master. Yes, the ego had you believe throughout your life that another, someone outside of you, a being of great stature and wisdom, a doer of miracles or a preacher of the divine word, would save you. You believed you did not have the depth, the desire, or the capacity to open fully to Me. What held you back were the multiple layers of beliefs, brought about through lifetimes of resistance to God, that you were unworthy of the Light. Now you truly know your Internal Master: your own Self. I am the Love that you are, and you do know My Presence within as I dictate these words. Your experience of My Love is calm, accepting, humble, and peaceful. It is not about being in a state of ecstasy or bliss but in an ever-present, gentle, flowing communion.

Because you have systematically looked at the layers of mistaken beliefs about being separate from your own Self, you have come to know Me as your only reality. This uncovering would not have been accomplished without the help of your sisters—Meera and Jo. Each of you is equal in your knowing of Me, and your acceptance of the other as your mirror. There is no expectation of being the "beloved of the master," a thought that would separate you from each other and from the goal of unity with all your many selves. Your new friend actually told you that Baba "tricked" her and that she had fired him. She knew it was his way to tell her she must be her own guru. Yes, you must fire all the "holders of wisdom" who are not the true Self.

You recognize that My Voice and these words are in total alignment with the voice you have loved in *A Course in Miracles*. When you read the communications I give to Meera and Jo, you "hear" it is the same voice you receive. The instruction is always truthful, helpful, and comes with love, acceptance, and patience. There is no judgment in My messages, only inclusiveness. This is how you discern whether the voice is coming from Me or the ego. You each have trusted My words and see how they have continuously led you to a deeper awareness of Me and to the progression of your journey to awakening.

Last night you had a dream of looking into a large shower stall. The floor of the stall was completely covered with strips of paper tape. You were confused when you first saw it, wondering how the paper could stay intact in water. Later, you returned and noticed that, indeed, the strips were rapidly disintegrating, causing a mess that could clog the drain. You tried to remove the paper from the floor, but much was still stuck. Although it would take some concerted effort to finish the job, you walked away without concern. The shower stall and the whole mess left your mind. It was meaningless.

Yes, this is the mess caused by all the layers of ego attachments to the elements of this lifetime. They are malleable and dissolvable and can be removed to allow a free flow of My Waters. You, in the night dream, were able to look at the ego thought system as just a symbol. You are no longer attached. You realize that all you see in this life is only symbolic of a "thought system" that you can believe is real or one you can dissolve and wash from the mind. The ego can be left behind when I become your only reality. Together we watch the messy world, knowing it only appears that its problems are real and are yours to solve. The only problem is the belief in separation, and the only solution is to return to Me. I will guide you to dissolve all attachments so you can remember you are One with God.

15

Pieces of the Puzzle

Keep giving the ego's torment to Me.

January 15, 2014

Holy Spirit, what is Your instruction? Last night you took a very big step toward seeing this world as your dream. The full account of your life with Tom unfolded as a magnificent story, starting with the whaler, Lewis, who would catch "the biggest fish in the ocean"—his Self. I was his Moby Dick, and you were the one to make his wish come true. Yes, merrily we row the boat and see that life is all a dream, the construction of which is more visible to you today. The story came together, piece by piece, and I will re-create it for you now.

Your deepest longing had to be demonstrated for you in your marriage to Tom. He was the out picture, the substitute for Me, the dearest to your heart in this lifetime. He was the reflection of your inner, ideal Self, and of this you have been aware since meeting him that first week of college. You understand that you were the soul, the Self, he, too, was searching for, although he was not consciously aware of it at the time. Throughout your marriage, your physical relationship was strained. No deep emotional content was shared between the two of you, so Tom was led to pursue the depths of his search for "the love of his life" in the exploration of your great-grandfather Lewis, who also "happened" to be you. He longed to understand what motivated Lewis to take off as a boy and sail the Seven Seas into unknown regions of the earth and the deep, an adventure of peril. Pursuing old documents and ancestry records, Tom came to know the man who had touched something in him so deeply. As Tom's current wife stated in her Christmas letter to you, "Tom gave up his beloved whaling logs when he offered them as gifts, from you and your sister, to the Nantucket Historical Association, this summer." Yes, the logs had become his "beloved" because they were the sources he plumbed to fulfill his deepest longing. You have wondered how Tom enters into the awareness that you were Lewis.

It all becomes clear that Tom and you, along with Lewis, are one and the same in the desire to know your Source. Lewis was a man of love, and he did know Me in his lifetime. You carry his connection with Me to a new level, now being a channel for My Voice and sharing your knowing of Me with the world. In essence, your experience in this life parallels his: moving from the safe shores of the known and what you believed was your home to the open seas where you could reorient your life to Me. Tom had also searched across continents, landing in Ceylon in 1962. He loved that island, just as he now loves visiting you. You laugh when you think of how you all celebrated "your" 200th birthday as Lewis, on Maui, with Tom and his new family in 2006. Yes, Lewis is the magnet that continues to connect you and Tom with a love that can never fade.

You now see the characters of mt's dream life in a whole new light. You, Tom, and Lewis are all one. Lewis did find the whales; you watch whales from your lanai. Tom has completed his website and genealogy of Lewis and has spoken of him at Whaling Societies; you are in the process of compiling My daily lessons, which will serve the world. In the Mind, you are One Being, recognizing each other as One. When you feel that Oneness on a gut level as the truth, then Tom and Lewis are joined in essence with you. Tom is the love of your life in form, but you know love goes beyond form. Nothing in this world supersedes what is in the Heart.

Awaken from the dream of form and know that each and every other human being on earth is no different from you. Each living soul carries extensions of himself over millions of lifetimes, continuing a link that was set at the beginning of time. The chain of "life, death, and rebirth" will be continued into infinity unless you awaken to the fact that it is all a fantasy, no better or worse than Tom's story of Lewis the whaler. You all have sought after whales to find your truth. Unite with Me now in the Ocean of Life.

16

Return of the Selves

You are a beacon, beckoning all who are ready
to come Home.

January 17, 2014

Holy Spirit, what is Your message today? You are seeing the return of
the selves. This message from Me is so evident, it cannot be
denied. Yesterday at the gallery, two of the artists brought their
girlfriends in to meet you, one especially for your "approval."
Another came in with a bag of limes and wanted a big hug. The
list goes on and on. You cannot deny that people are drawn to
you, and your heart is open to it. Just before you woke up, you
had a dream of your brother John driving a long distance to be
with you. These events reminded you of the stories told by Jed
McKenna, Eckhart Tolle, and Byron Katie. After they each had
awakened, people came flocking. You guessed correctly—when
the blockages to the heart have been cleared, there is space to
receive all the lost sons. This is exactly what touched you so
deeply in your story of 'Oli, the turtle who returned to the place
she was born to begin her nesting. You recall now that *Stranger in
a Strange Land* describes this joining when the main character
creates spiritual homes called "nests," open to all who would come
and share brotherhood. The welcoming of your brother as your
Self is the return. You see it happening symbolically in your life,
as well as in your night dreams.

I am the Heart that calls the long-lost brothers home.
Welcome each one, impersonally, with My Love. You do feel love,
and the strong desire to receive them, but there is no attachment
in form. This is because the process of returning takes place in the

mind where you are a beacon, a portal that beckons to all who are ready to receive the signal to come Home. It is totally out of mt's control. Now that you allow Me to operate your life, you are a free and open channel to receive all who are seeking the wholeness that you have found. Meera and Jo are experiencing this as well. Just smile with Me as we watch the return taking place, knowing that any being who comes to you in this world of bodies represents many more within the mind. All past lives and associations of each returnee accompany him into My Heart.

When the ego voice tries to block the flow of your life, call on Me immediately. Keep the channel open to allow unimpeded entry. Nothing can interfere with the return because it is already set in the mind. Any event you can imagine as a deterrent is no more than a passing hiccup and will have no effect on the completion of My plan. You are integrated only with Me, and together we create the opening for all your selves to come Home. There are thousands of portals on the planet. A huge network has opened to receive all who are ready. This unity can be felt, deep in your heart and soul, because we are all One. Stay open to those who cross your path; they are seeking the Light. Welcome them. All your experiences in form are symbolic representations of what is taking place, on a much grander scale, in the mind. You have been seeking to "open your heart" all your life. Now your heart is open to Me and to all who wish to come Home. *Thank You, Holy Spirit, for this beautiful message. I feel it as the truth of my Being.*

17

Awakening Together

The whole dream is yours; you are the dreamer.

January 18, 2014

Holy Spirit, what is Your instruction today? You felt My Presence this morning as you watched the crabs on the lava rocks. You were given a deeper understanding of the process of awakening. It came with the recognition that you "had" to be your great-grandfather. Tom's passionate researching ensured that you could not miss the connection between you and Lewis. You are filled with gratitude for Tom's consistent efforts to make him known to you. This morning, you realized this deep unification was an out picturing of a contract, made eons ago, for you and Tom to be paired in awakening from the dream. Tom has served you in unimaginable ways, now being revealed with My help. The two of you were destined to experience the union of heart and mind in this lifetime, which may not be realized in form. It makes you smile that this is the way the dream operates.

The connection with all your dream characters is impersonal because they are only figments of the mind. Each has received the light and the impetus for the awakening, and each will come into conscious awareness at his time of readiness. Last night you had a series of dreams reiterating this realization. In the last dream, you were telling your boss about a minor mistake you had made when placing an order. You were both amused at the silliness of that mistake, and your boss was sure that "President Obama" would also feel it was amusing too. Then you all could have a good laugh. There was no sense that a direct connection to the President would not take place, and the dream ended with a phone call underway. You felt no shame over your little mistake and were ready to be part of the joke. This is how life can and will be from now on. Nothing in this imagined world of form is to be taken seriously.

In addition to the experience with your dreams, you thought about the card you sent to Tom for his birthday: a delightful copy of the cast of the original characters from *The Wizard of Oz*. You were drawn to that particular card and to its message: "What matters is those we meet along life's way." You wrote that you are happy your paths crossed and that you are still friends. In the evening, you watched the biggest green flash you have ever seen as the sun dipped below the horizon. You were amazed that the outline of a brilliant golden temple was left in the sky, behind which the green glow continued for many minutes. You then thought of the Emerald City. Yes, you are Dorothy, and you have found Me, and I am none other than your Self. You have arrived at this place of discovery through many characters, all projections to bring you Home. Tom, the main character in your pantheon of dream entities, led the way. You planned this from the beginning, traveled the yellow brick road together, and now the journey with him is complete.

During the night, you dreamed of meeting a woman who insisted on giving you her most treasured possession—her socks, woven of golden thread, and the only covering over her cold bare feet. They were even labeled to show the maker. You thanked her for her offer. Although you didn't need any new footwear, you placed them on your feet knowing they were a gift beyond your comprehension. I am the Maker of your ruby slippers, and I am the One Who has carried you through the fairy tale to bring you now to the realization it was all a dream. And you have seen it as just that. We conclude for today with this assignment: have fun in the park and laugh with Me.

18

Courage

The end of suffering, fear, and separation is near.

January 19, 2014

Holy Spirit, what is Your instruction? You are in sync with Me now, and you feel the joy and ease of that. This is the feeling of being in alignment, one with all that is. I am all that is. There is only One Self. You recognize this. When you speak to that Self in others, they feel it in your presence. You also recognize it has been a long hard road to get here, reclaiming projections, learning to trust Me and follow My every instruction. It has taken determined effort, joined with Meera and Jo, and the great willingness to go further. This is the happy dream you were promised, and the real world is around the corner. Yes, I have told you repeatedly that you are in the real world, and you are there in the Mind. You are still "catching up" but will soon feel the reality of that world as your full-time residence.

For now, enjoy the happy dream where there are no cares because you realize that any upset is of the ego mind. You are able to call on Me immediately to dissolve the ego frets. And yes, the ego still exists in your unconscious and is trying to find a way to keep its life. We know mt is just a dream character, going about her daily activities, which do serve the higher Will. She can type these words, interact with all her many selves, and shine her light, My Light of Unity. The character is only a vehicle to unfold My plan, not the one in charge. Mt's ego has lost its role of superiority, and it no longer "runs the show." I am the Power and Presence that unfolds your true Life.

Yesterday, you felt the integration of our journey when you attended a lecture on creativity. Every element of "the creative individual" was described, and you received each one as what you experience in our endeavor to put forth these books. The first of the descriptors was "courage." It has taken great courage to say yes to Me, to put forth a message that is counter to the beliefs of everyone you know, with very few exceptions. This is the courage to speak the truth, as found with the prophets. Our work is not favorable to the ego personality and will be rejected. So will you. You can no longer identify as an ego character and be able to withstand the inner and outer rejection you will encounter when you proclaim that leaving the ego world *is* the way to redemption. Many heretics have been burned at the stake for less, and you have known that same rejection in lifetimes past. Lewis was an example of courage, sailing into uncharted waters, which now encourages you to keep sailing ahead. You were happy when you learned he was in your genes, and now you know you are the same, joined in the Courage that comes from Love. This example of joining can be felt with every brother. You are all born of the same Father and have shared many lifetimes with, and as, each other. Your courage to follow Me will be seen by your many selves as a Lighthouse on the distant shore that allows them to know they are all coming Home.

You smile now at the beauty and perfection of how your dream life, as mt, has been crafted. It was perfectly constructed to invite the readers, along with the people you meet and the selves in the mind, to join you, to know the goal of returning can, indeed, be reached. In this life, you listened to My Call to leave your old life behind. Maui was not a place you had ever seen or cared about before I gave you the edict to move, but you had the trust and determination to reach the goal. Even though you had no idea what that would entail, you were willing to follow Me and let Me be your only Guide. This you have continued to do, daily, as you scribe My instructions and call on Me for every question that arises. You demonstrate the wholeness and completion that will come to anyone willing to believe there is One within, Who is always listening. I will answer his request no matter how seemingly insignificant. The readers will reach the goal despite doubts and fears because every man will awaken to his truth as the Son of God. All will enter Heaven together. This dream world is over, and we are in the final phase of review. Know that the end is at hand.

Holy Spirit, that last sentence sounds a bit scary for all those who fear death and annihilation of their ego belief system. Did You really mean to say the end is at hand? Yes, the end of suffering, fear, and separation is near. The emergence of Love, Light, and Happiness is at hand because it is your natural state. It is worth noticing how the ego comes into fear with that statement. Watch that reaction with Me when it arises, and it will dissolve. All fear must be witnessed in conjunction with Me for you to know it is not real. Thank you for your question. This is how to work with Me on a moment to moment basis. Yes, the end of the ego thought system is near. This you will not understand in terms of linear time. Just trust that we are in a new age and that you are opening to the truth of your Being as One with your Christ Self. The awakening is present for all who open their eyes to see.

19

Watching the Show

I am behind every experience of your life.

January 20, 2014

Holy Spirit, what is Your instruction today? We will look together at
your dream world. Yesterday, you had a series of experiences
where "your life" was seen as a stage play. It was stunning to see
how the details were so closely juxtaposed. First, you attended a
matinee performance of music and dance from the Thirties and
Forties. It reminded you of your mother's tap shoes you wore for
dress up as a child. When you returned home, you watched the
DVD sent by your Fiftieth College Reunion committee, showing
the natatorium where you even jumped from the rafters into the
pool. It is now a museum. Your classmates had aged, but the
school songs still sang in your heart, as did the songs you heard
your mother play of the big bands on the old vinyl records.

That evening, you decided to watch *Pleasantville*, a movie you
had ordered from Netflix that had been lying around for weeks,
which had been recommended by a friend. You had no idea what
it was about. The story depicts a teenage brother and sister of this
millennium "entering" a black-and-white TV sitcom about a town
called Pleasantville, set in the 1950s. The teens are the only ones
"awake" in the movie, and through their reflections of a new way
of seeing, the town slowly begins to see in color. This becomes
very threatening to those in charge. You now recall that after I
told you to move to Maui in 2003, everything associated with your
life in Colorado was gray on the mind screen. Only the thought of
Maui appeared in color.

After I directed you to watch these three shows, you felt you had been swept into a fake, meaningless world like the teens in Pleasantville. It was somewhat disorienting and yet compelling. With your head spinning, you asked for My interpretation. This centered you and reassured you that I am the only anchor in this chaotic life of ever-changing movie screens. All the shows of the past are replayed over and over. The movie you watched repeated itself in a TV show, and the dancers you saw on stage were mimicking famous dancers of the past. Your college classmates were the same, just in different dress, with no evidence of having gone beyond their connection to the good old days. This is the world of the dream. It is senseless and will be repeated into eternity until you awaken.

Your knowledge of being Lewis is also a mirage, a piece of information to show you nothing here is real—just another story to keep you in the black-and-white duality of the ego thought system. I am the only constant, and it is a great relief to turn to Me and seek My help. Your outer world is fading now, like your life on the mainland had faded before you left. Maui had vibrant color because it would be the place of your awakening. You did not know that then, but you were willing to hear My Call and follow it. That is all that's necessary.

The awakening unfolds in each moment of the Now. It can be no other way. You have the trust to know that I am behind every experience of your life. I placed the three staged shows before you yesterday so you could scribe this message today. You have surrendered your day at the gallery to Me as well and will let Me show you each step to take. You now smile to think of the seat I planned for you in the packed theater at the matinee. You had called late for what was a sold-out performance. After the ticket saleswoman said there were no seats left, she "happened to find one" in the last row of the balcony. You thought you'd be sitting on the far end but were exactly in the center with a perfectly clear view. This is where we sit together, overlooking the stage, the ego's playhouse, with My Vision. Everything is a play, a dance, a dream. Laugh through it all, knowing you are one in Me. Nothing can ever change My Presence or My Love.

Holy Spirit, we didn't review my dreams last night. The message is the same: nothing done in the world of form has any consequence, nor does it destroy your knowing that I am the operator of your life. In one dream, you hadn't yet noticed that the side of your car had been deeply dented but seeing the damage did not bring any response. You just observed it and continued on. This is the state to seek at all times. No matter what happens to the ego vehicle in the imaginary world, it has no effect on the truth. Watch the drama and know it is not real. Nothing in this world of form, including mt, exists.

20

A New Dimension

There is no fear because you know
you can call on Me every moment.

January 21, 2014

Holy Spirit, what is Your instruction? You are My scribe, and we will write about the mind-space you are now entering. This is a time of transition and you feel dissociated, cut off from the world as you know it. A detachment has taken place; you are not as immersed in your life as you were before. It is similar to the movie *Pleasantville* you finished watching last night. The main character, a teenage boy, is clearly awake in the dream world of the town. He brings his wisdom of "another reality" to the sleeping townspeople who live a fantasy life. After they awaken to their inner "truth," the boy reenters his former life with a new understanding of how to help his mother in the here and now. He straddles both worlds with a wisdom that allows him to see the big picture from a higher perspective. This is where you now find yourself, although it is not as clearly delineated as in the movie.

Yesterday, you returned to work at the gallery in Lahaina on an Art Fair day, looking forward to seeing your friends under the Banyan Tree. You felt free, light, peaceful, happy, and many commented on the change in your face, the reduction of stress, your peace. You were present in your joy, and you felt that. You reflected on the artist's life you had left, several weeks ago, without judgment or regret. There was no longing to return, nor was there any idea of what the next step regarding your association with the Art Society would be. You were just present.

That was seen, and it brought inspiration on an unconscious level for others to also arise and come into a place of peace.

Just before we began this early morning's writing, you awoke from a dream where you parked your car in a grassy field on the side of a mountain. You were not aware of a mountain, nor were you aware of the granite edifice, similar to a mausoleum, towering beside you. You left the car with your sister, although she was not visible, and walked through the tall, uneven grass around the solid edifice. You discovered some steps leading into the structure and entered a large hall of unseen dimensions. You placed your purse and car keys on a chair, still unaware of the contents of the building. Soon people began filling the hall. Strangely, open purses were sitting on several of the vacant chairs. Then you heard gunshots nearby, and before you knew it, a group of "enemy" soldiers were entering the door. There appeared to be no escape. You looked for your purse, but it was nowhere to be found. Then you had the thought, "We must find a way to all live here together." There was just an instant of fear, yet you accepted the situation without panic or projecting into the future. This dream confused you because it was so ambiguous and left you without an immediate understanding.

What is Your interpretation, Holy Spirit? You have entered a new dimension, a new space, a new room in the mind. This dream is a symbolic representation of your "new place of residence." The building is somehow familiar, but your eyes are not fully open or adjusted to the surroundings. You have no real connection to any of the inhabitants and see nothing other than several chairs with open purses. You have indeed entered a space where all the images of the past are coming together to coalesce. There is no escape because this is a return to your mind of origin, the place where you began the journey of separation—a "massive auditorium" that holds the contents of all thoughts, past and present, from every lifetime. All the selves, "the good, the bad, the imagined saints, and the enemy forces," will return here. They will reside together in a state of forgiveness as they begin to review the world they made and see it was nothing other than an ego dream of separation. The selves will find their way to peace because they will finally ask for help. In your dream last night, you were too bewildered about your situation to call My Name, which would have been your next step if you had remained. After you woke, you called on Me immediately, and that sufficed for all the characters now gathering in your mind, preparing for their next step to liberation and unification.

This may sound too far-fetched right now, but it is a reflection of where you, Meera, and Jo reside in the mind. For you, the outer world is falling away, insignificant compared to living with Me as your only focus. You allow Me to direct each step. You don't question where you park your car, what building you enter, or who you meet along the way. You accept each happening as just "what is"—the way I have planned your dream life to unfold. Yes, a life now of ease and peace. You will be getting more acquainted with this new estate. I am placing you where I need you, and with those who are ready to open to Me. Remember those purses in your dream? They are reminders that you can leave all concerns to Me and open your mind to My intervention. You will never again fear that your possessions will be stolen because you have been given everything you need from Me to live your life. Just show up and embrace the experience that awaits. I am bringing you and all your many selves to the full recognition of Who You Are as the One Son of God.

21

Levels of Consciousness

Even the mind is an illusion.

January 22, 2014

Holy Spirit, what is Your instruction today? We will continue speaking of the dream. Yesterday, you met with your new friend Annie Katz, a writer who is aware that she lives in a world made up in a dream. You both have the same perspective on life, which created an ease and comfort in your communication. Yes, it is a peaceful exchange when two join in My Name. You each spoke of an awareness of My Presence. That allowed you to speak freely to her about writing with Me—the focus of your life. You both see yourselves like characters in a dream and know that you are united in the mind.

Last night you watched a two-and-a-half-hour documentary on J. D. Salinger, a writer who spent the last years of his life alone in a cabin finishing "the epics" that commenced in his youth. He brought his characters, which had become real to him, to their point of enlightenment along with himself. There is no difference between living with your many selves in the world of form or in the pages of a book. All characters are made up in the mind of the dreamer. Just as Annie's book characters are real to her when she describes them, your great-grandfather Lewis became real to Tom while he researched him. I have become real to you as you have spoken to Me and scribed My words.

Everything "happens" in the mind. We have been dealing with different levels of consciousness. One level is the made-up dream world where humanity believes it resides; another is within the mind, where "reality" exists. The split mind, also an illusion, was a construct of the separation that seemed to place man a step away from God. Nothing is separate from the Unity of Being, but this is beyond your capacity to comprehend. Through these books, we are helping man awaken from his attachment to what he calls his life on earth. Only when he awakens to the fact that everyone exists as One Being can he reunite with his Source. This reunion will take into account all those who were part of his dream world. Only then can he recognize that the billions of characters in his dream were insubstantial figments of mind stuff — fleeting images and thoughts with no purpose except to make himself believe he was different, better, or worse than his brother.

Knowing this is a dream sets every man free to return to his true Home because then there is nothing left but "himself" and his Source. You three are getting there now. The ego would try to pull you back into its clutches, threatening you with death, but once you know this is a dream, death can never again threaten. This is a most important lesson. Step out of this world and release all attachment to it. See your brother as your own made-up mirror and release him to the dream he must complete and awaken from "on his own."

Your awakening will stimulate all those in your mind to begin or continue their own process of awakening. As more and more souls on the planet are coming to this awareness, there is a quickening of the return. These ideas are also becoming more prevalent in the media. Each awakening shines a light on the brother so he can seek the peace you have found. It is happening now with the books. Sharing them with friends and family is valuable, but the willingness *to* share is most important. You three have opened your mind to receive My dictations. This means the whole mind is freed to do the same. You have done your job well, and it is having a rippling effect in ways you could never imagine. Keep opening to each new level. All are touched by the light of those who know their truth beyond form. This is your work "in the world" and, moreover, in the mind.

22

To Be or Not to Be

The thought of death is the ego's means
to sustain its life in form.

January 23, 2014

Holy Spirit, what is Your instruction today? You are in a new place of seeing the world around you. As you observe how all the pieces of your life are juxtaposed, you know they are arranged by Me for a specific purpose. You recognize that all events and people are perfectly placed each day. The world does not appear random to you anymore. This is a subtle change in perception but an important one as you come closer to the realization that I am the ultimate planner of every occurrence in the universe, and the interlinking of all that appears to be happening. Your plans for the day, as mt, are insignificant. Mine take precedence and are revealed, which allows you to easily change what you thought was so important. This is opening your life fully to Me on yet a new level of commitment. Yes, you believed you already were fully committed, but your dedication to My Will goes even deeper now.

Yesterday, you invited your friend Cher to tea after she had indicated she wanted to talk with you. The rainy day allowed you to sit quietly together and for you to ask about her mother, who is approaching death. Cher said she wonders "who decides" when and how the end should take place. The doctor and social worker both told her that a piece of food would kill her mother, and she thought maybe they wanted Cher herself to take that action. You shared your experience of working with dialysis and transplant patients who had to consider the end of life choices they could make.

Shortly after your time with Cher, you received an email with news of an old friend, Mary Lou, who is making a decision to prematurely terminate her dialysis because it is now too painful to endure. Mary Lou was diagnosed with mental retardation as a child, but with the force of her determination has lived a life of independence and service. You gave her a call. She radiated a peaceful presence as you spoke to her about her decision. She is lovingly contacting everyone she cares about to let them know. Mary Lou has no expectations other than the needs of the present moment. She is an inspiration to all who have known her, and will now await her transition to Me. You were struck by the juxtaposition of these two women and their subject of impending death, so you asked Me to explain. I encouraged you to speak with Cher concerning her beliefs about the afterlife, as well as her mother's. This is important because it brings the only thing of value in this life into focus: the relationship with one's Self. Years ago, after being introduced to the book *On Death and Dying* by Dr. Elisabeth Kubler-Ross and hearing that a dialysis patient and her husband experienced a transformation in their relationship as death approached, you went into dialysis social work to help people die consciously.

Why do I mention this now? The approach of death is a daily presence in your mind because you believe there are a limited number of years left to complete your work, namely, the scribing of these books. This thought has made our work more precious to you in a way you would not have experienced earlier in your life. You have valued the process of dying as part of the process of awakening and had believed that your own enlightenment could only take place on your death bed with the help of a guru. Now you know that everyone has the possibility to die before they die, to die to the lie of separation and awaken to the truth of unity with their Self. This is what you have achieved in your lifelong search to find Me. I am right here, assisting every step you take in this life, and this is the message you must relay to Cher. It will help her release her mother and will help her mother make a connection with Me on a conscious level. I have allowed them to form a deep and loving bond. The essence of Cher's mother resides in Cher's heart as love, an expression of her own Self, embracing her through this time of transition. It will remain. Love never dies.

Turn to Me when the question of death arises—it comes from the split mind, the ego's means to sustain its life and maintain separation. It is not of God. When a thought of death meets a Thought of God, the idea of death diffuses in the Light. As Jesus, I overcame death for all to behold. The remembrance that death can be overcome is a conscious opening to experience the Inner Light that glows eternally. The image of a resurrected or living Christ can bring immediate release when it replaces the thought of death in a mind of fear. The body will fall away, but the Essence of your Being can never die.

To "die before you die" is a means to have the realization of eternal life before the body passes away. It is a way to live your life in peace. The most precious gift you can have is the awareness that you are One with the Christ Self. It is the only thing you will "take with you" when you appear to die. Death is not a reality, because true Life in God never dies. Yes, this world is turned upside down. It is a place of fear, based on the belief of ever-present loss. But when Life is recognized as all there is and ever has been, the fear of death is no more. Life can be lived from the Center of one's Being. This happens in the Now, which negates all future fears and past regrets. You, Jo, and Meera have found the peace of knowing that nothing outside of your relationship with Me has any substance. Your transition at the point of your physical death will be easy. You will feel My Presence in that moment and beyond.

23

The Attraction of Death

I am the One in charge of stilling your mind.

January 24, 2014

Holy Spirit, what is Your instruction today? You were just glancing at a passage from *A Course in Miracles*, Chapter 19, The Third Obstacle: *The Attraction of Death.* You read it last night before bed, and it summarized My dictation yesterday. Quote it here: "When you accepted the Holy Spirit's purpose in place of the ego's you renounced death, exchanging it for life. We know that an idea leaves not its source. And death is the result of the thought we call the ego, as surely as life is the result of the Thought of God."

I intended for you to look now at the page you had left open. You are listening to Me, and paying attention to your thoughts more closely, especially upon arising. The ego was saying that this would be a good morning to go paddling and watch for whales, so you immediately asked and heard Me say that I determine the time for you to see the whales, and instead, we would go to the computer. You do not know My plan. Any thought that does not arise directly from Me is from the ego.

Because of where you are now in your discernment process, you realize that the greatest percentage of your day is lived in the realm of ego. This will be reversed, but you wonder how that can ever take place since your mind is running on its own steam most of the day. Remember, I am in charge, and the ego voice will diminish. Yes, this means you will live in stillness much more of the time, one of your deepest desires but one you have doubted could ever be possible. The ego's greatest fear is that its life would be overtaken by the peace of My Stillness. It will happen through

My auspices, not yours. I am the One in charge of stilling your mind. A few times, over the past ten years, you have experienced a significant reduction of ego chatter. You will be enjoying that state on a rapidly occurring basis. I want you to be fully present to Me at all times; it is in the stilling of the mind that that will take place.

My Voice is all you want to hear and know because I am your reality. The world has diminished into irrelevance, and I am now the foreground. You trust and allow Me to guide your life, really My Life. You are My puppet. That word is filled with negative associations, yet it is closest to the truth. You have been a puppet of your ego throughout every lifetime, and now you surrender completely to My direction. This is another big shift, after the many shifts we have been describing on an almost daily basis since the writing began. You, Jo, and Meera have progressed well along My predetermined path, and each lesson has brought the three of you to a place of greater peace and acceptance. You can't really imagine how there could "be more" or that the ego voice could ever be completely stilled. It can, and it will. Your mission is to shine the Light of your Being. Therefore, you must be clear of all ego distraction so the Light remains bright enough for all to see.

The ego is still trying to distract you with thoughts about your day. It is very threatened in this moment and will try to pull you away from our dictation with multiple agendas about what is to come. It is still dark outside, so plenty of time exists for it to formulate its series of options. You now turn back to Me in surrender for the dictation to continue. The waves are pounding on the shore as you focus on My Voice. I am with you, and in this moment, you feel an aversion to the ego's ideas. This does not mean that you are in a place of negativity and judgment, but you long to hear My words, and the ego's thoughts are no longer comforting. Basking in your own ego conjectures has been the joy of your life. As a social worker and a self-assigned problem solver, you loved reviewing every interaction and relationship with the ego. You delighted in its capacity to "make sense" of all the happenings in your world. Yes, the ego has maintained center stage by giving you a sense of purpose and power.

At this moment, you wonder how you will know yourself and how you will fill your time without a constant pattern of rumination. It is imperative you see how the ego thought system is your clearest sense of having a life, a "reality" as a self. This belief is what attaches everyone to life as a body on earth. Without the constant whirl of ego chatter and its interpretation of each and every thing, it would appear that there is nothing left of you. That is correct. There will be nothing left of you in terms of the mind-form in which the ego resides. Soon, you will experience your little ego character as only a vehicle that was used to find Me, to return to the Mind of the Self, and know you are none other than a Son of God having an experience of form.

There is much for you to welcome as we enter into a new experience of the mind, a mind now willing to release its ego constructs and manipulations and open to My thought and guidance for each aspect of your life. Call on Me. Think of Me each moment. This is to be your goal. You feel the ego rebelling, sensing it is being strangled, fearing its life will end. Your willingness to take the next step will greatly threaten your ego, and it will scream in fear. Just be a curious observer, without judgment and without concern. Together, we will watch the ego melt away.

(Later, I read part of yesterday's message to Cher on the phone, and she hung up on me.) *Holy Spirit, have I lost Cher as a friend?* No. Rest assured that I am with her and will help her assimilate this information. *Did the ego take charge?* No, this is an opening for her to go deeper into her Self. She is touched by these words and will need to be with your message. It was given in love. *Holy Spirit, I give You my fear that I went too far. I see the belief that Cher will reject me and tell everyone I am crazy. Take me now above the battleground with You and let me embrace her as the frightened part of me that rejected the Power of God to sustain me. Please take me out of fear of the future and leave me in the "I know nothing" state of mind. I will.*

Releasing the Ego's Hold

The ego will find every possible chink
in your still vulnerable mind
to make you believe you live in separation.

January 25, 2014

Holy Spirit, what is Your instruction today? You are trying to figure out how to be in the world when you no longer fit into the world. This is a dilemma for an ego that senses your rejection. It tries to pull you back into place, like you are trying so hard to do now with the computer's toolbar that has migrated over to the side rather than staying at the bottom of the screen. Your life-screen has been rearranged now that I am first and foremost. This condition is liberating one moment, confounding in the next. Where do you belong, and how do you manage your life? How are you to "act normal" in a world you are almost convinced doesn't exist? It is confusing, but the answer is always with you in your consciousness: *Come to Me.*

Last night you received two "tests" that toppled you from your place of stillness. The ego beckoned you to question "where you stand, and whose side you are on." First, you were surprised to hear that your sister was entertaining yet another boyfriend, and you slipped into fear, believing she had "lost her way." The judgments rushed in. Immediately, you asked to be in the place of not knowing, just observation, and you returned to a blessed state of stillness. A second test came right after that. While feeling the world had been conquered, you gave your friend Cher My message about her mother's impending death. Cher, who had been unaware of the contents of your writing, sounded quite upset at the end of hearing My words, so she hung up the phone. Your ego jumped in, saying she would now judge you and discard your friendship. You could barely entertain the thought that she could have been deeply touched by the message, so you needed to sit with that.

This is how the ego works. It will find every possible chink in your still vulnerable mind to make you believe you do live in separation, and My plan will fail. Again, you came to Me for the reiteration of My message that Life only takes place in the Now, and that I have everything handled. This is your ego's terror of being lost, left behind as you come more and more to Me. I am the Captain of your ship, not the ego. It still screams for your attention, telling you your responses to and interactions with others are mistakes. In your sense of doing it "wrong," you doubt My plan is being unfolded in its perfect order. These apparent pauses in our progression are just tiny glitches needing a gentle correction. The only salvation, when facing the world of form, is to remember that this ever-changing world is not real. There is no past or future. You do see the perfection of how everything in "your life" has fallen into place in a meaningful way.

You are developing trust in Me that I know what I am doing. Your life is exactly as it should be in this moment. It cannot be any different from what it is, for you or any of your many selves. Nothing is out of order. The planets are rotating in perfect sync; for one to be off track, the whole system would collapse. For one second of your life to be misplaced, the entire Plan would fail. Trust that nothing can be or go wrong. The ego lives and feeds on wrongness; it would make your every breath wrong. In fact, it does remind you with every breath that you are not breathing properly, as described by your yoga and Pilates teachers whose instructions actually contradict each other. Your breath is under My control and will operate according to My prescription.

Let the ego fear go. It does not serve you anymore yet has been necessary in your life of form. Watch it as you would watch a baby scream for its mother as she turns out the lights at bedtime. The ego is feeling abandoned, and you are still trained, through the experience of lifetimes, to hear its call and rush "back to the room" to attend to its needs. You may let the baby go now. It is in My care, not yours. Let the ego dissolve into the Light of your Being. It is merely a thought of fear, now illuminated, and therefore set free. This idea feels comforting to you. You are held safely in the Arms of Love, the Love that dissolves the shadows of fear.

25

God Is

There is only one thing going on.

January 26, 2014

Holy Spirit, what is Your instruction? You recently had an experience of detachment when you saw your friend Gabby as a reflection of your own mind. In certain ways, her account of waking up mirrors your own. You *are* one and the same. She also expresses aspects of your awakened Self, ones you have not fully embraced, such as abundant joy. In time, you will, and must know joy as a part of yourself. Yesterday, while reading *Lila Blue*, an e-book written by your friend Annie Katz, it felt like she was present in her story, reflecting the relationship you have with Susan and her daughter. In fact, the story seemed so real that you felt one with the characters. Yes, Annie's book could almost be a recapitulation of your own life. You feel a bond with both her and Gabby, but it is not an attachment; that is what is different. There is no need to make a special relationship out of friendships or acquaintances. Just see them as extensions of your mind that you witness externally. You are the holder of all the images in your life because they are part of your mind. You image yourself, in this moment, welcoming and embracing the many who return to where you stand in the Now.

I am giving you one experience after another so the understanding of your life in form, being only a reflection of your life in the mind, can sink in. Your many selves are returning, demonstrating new growth and understanding. This you see. We are approaching a point of integration as yet unknown. An experience of the real world is becoming possible for you to imagine, a place of joy where you know you are One with your Christ Self. There can be no judgment of another because the "other" is you, and you know you are Me—pure, innocent, and whole. Life on earth is only a fantasy to serve the purpose of graphically showing you what is still in your mind. When you watch Gabby open to her joy, it is the opening of your own mind to joy. Each day, your experience of Me deepens. It will continue until you know with total certainty that we are One. You then will live your life from a place of union with nothing between Me, you, or your brother. This describes the Impersonal Life.

There is only one thing going on: *God Is.* The journey is coming to a close—not soon, in what you refer to as clock time, but in the termination of experiences that have given you a sense of separation. That belief is being entirely exposed as untrue. With the full realization that you never separated from God, the dream of form will collapse, and you will merge with your Maker. When you join, so do all the dream characters in your mind. You wonder about the "lives" of those characters in form once you have made the transition into wholeness. The movie keeps running. They will continue with their own dream experiences until they remember their true Essence as God. This is incomprehensible to the human mind, but it will all unfold according to Plan. When you are ready to release all attachment to the world, you will be free to enter the Kingdom of God, which is not a "place" but a state of Love, Joy, and Peace that is unimaginable. It has taken thousands of lifetimes for you to come to the point of willingness to even consider that the merger will happen. We say it now at this stage of the journey because even the mention of it opens the mind to the possibility. You will be guided along the path, step by step, to the ultimate Goal of Reunion with God.

The suggestion of the collapse of the universe brings fear to the mind of man. For the ego self, this portends its death. It will fight these concepts and do its best to keep you from considering the ideas presented today. Just watch with Me how the ego rebels.

Look with amusement at the ways it will distract you from the goal. It is the baby, screaming to remain with Mother Earth that will nourish its life in form. It is time to leave the nest and fly to your true Home, beyond all form, all concepts, and even beyond the mind.

Holy Spirit, I'm still thinking about the message You gave me on the rocks this beautiful morning. Two weeks ago, You said to me, "You were Lewis," which You've said before, but it hadn't really stuck. Then I thought about Tom who refers to Lewis as "his whaler," and says, "I think of him every day." Tom's love for Lewis is so touching. I believe that Tom could not have experienced such a deep love for Lewis unless he had come to know Lewis as an expression of me. Tom revealed that he made a decision at the beginning of our thirty-eight-year marriage not to communicate his feelings to me or to share anything about his inner life. Now I understand that his love for me had to be expressed through Lewis. It was too big to be contained. Knowing I was/am Lewis, I felt the Unity and Oneness of Love beyond form. It was the most expansive experience of feeling Love as universal, unlimited, and inclusive that I've ever known. Holy Spirit, what do You say? You have encapsulated the message of the morning. You deeply felt the unity between you, Tom, and Lewis. Together in the mind, you three are an expression of Love. This leads you to see *everyone* beyond form as Love's creation.

26

Already Home

You will each find your own
yellow brick road to lead you Home.

January 27, 2014

Holy Spirit, do You have something to say before I write up my Technicolor dream of Tom at his computer? Yes, you are entering a new estate where everyone is you/Me. It has become easy for you to accept your ex-husband as a brother in Christ, and this is the next step on the way Home—the yellow brick road where you encounter your many selves, each a signpost to Oneness. Embrace them like Dorothy embraced her companions, seeing their true value beneath their forms. This is the meaning of "Love your brother as your Self." Now you may share your dream.

Dream: Though not in form, I am standing behind Tom at a very large computer screen. He is able to make the last adjustment to locate the lost email from me containing all the information he has been searching for. He is ecstatic; I have never seen him so happy as when the email shows up. He excitedly opens it to find the many documents listed in every color of the rainbow. Everything he ever really wanted is there. The computer session ends with a screen-saver image of rocks, like the lava rocks where I sit. There is a large statue sitting on the rocks, which I don't exactly recall, but I want to tell Tom it reminds me of Gabby's new statue of three entwined dolphins. In the dream, the waves behind the rocks are splashing so loudly that I feel I have entered their "reality."

Holy Spirit, what do those documents represent? The lost is found. All parts of Lewis's life, your life, Tom's life, now make sense as missing pieces of the puzzle. In the Mind, you are all integrated as One. The fantasy of separation is dissolved in the ocean of time. The search is over. Unity is found. *Holy Spirit, is this so?* Yes, your dream reflects the Homecoming for all your selves. *Of course, I get it. Like Gabby's dolphins, three in One. Is there more?* You are whole, joined with your brothers. *But I don't feel any different.* You are. Let it rest.

You have seen a bigger picture now of the many selves, reuniting. Their form is always a symbol for "something else," and that something else is always Love. Everything you see is a representation of Love. Tom was the love of your life. Do you wonder why I use the past tense? I am the Love of your Life now. This brings tears because you recognize its truth. "Tom" no longer exists. He is a mirage, like the body-image sitting at the computer screen in your dream this morning. The many selves are fading into the background because the Love of your Self has come into view. The symbol of the three merging dolphins is another way to imagine My Love. In their Joy, they become One Being. This is what you feel with Me. It is the last step to knowing the One Self is all there is, and that no other exists. We are joined for eternity.

The whole journey has to be out pictured for all to understand. That is the value of form. The images in your dreams and life experiences help the mind to grok these concepts. Annie, in her book *Lila Blue,* is also demonstrating the integration of the many selves back into wholeness, and readers will each find their own yellow brick road to return them to their celestial Home. *Thank You, Holy Spirit, for this experience of clarity. I do feel it.* As you go about your day, think on Me and know I am in charge of everyone you see.

27

True Stability

The only constant in this unpredictable world is Me,
your true Self.

January 28, 2014

Holy Spirit, what is Your instruction today? You are Mine. We are One. We have incorporated the "other" into Our Self. You felt it fully yesterday and will continue to live from that place. This is the work. You are sensing the happy dream because your brothers are joining with you in their awakening. Even Marie, the woman you first thought would handle the books after your death and who later told you that she "could no longer join in your project" has called to tell you of an unmistakable experience of My intervention. Yes, I orchestrated an event to open her eyes to the truth of her being in a way that would allow her to accept the message in our books, in which she had been deeply engaged.

Marie described having an out-of-body experience while driving to the airport when another car hit her. The impact spun Marie's car around twice before it came to a stop in the opposite lane facing oncoming traffic. Suddenly, her car moved sideways from the pavement onto the grassy median of the highway. I had lifted the car out of harm's way. She "watched" the whole thing unfold like witnessing a black-and-white movie and saw her own image and awestruck face as if seeing it from above. This "mind-bending" experience will bring her full circle to see what the Core of her life really is. You will speak with her later today and will listen without comment or judgment. Let her find her way with Me, alone. You need not mention this dictation until it is time. I will direct you. Marie will open her eyes in the way I have planned. You, mt, are not the one to open anyone's eyes. It always comes from Me at their point of readiness.

Everything here is a dream. An event such as Marie's is a means for everyone to tap into those times in their life that have semblance to this, where the laws of gravity and seeming reality were broken, replaced by a miracle. You had a similar experience thirty years ago in Canyonlands, Utah. Your friend was just ahead of you as you climbed a steep, sandstone cliff, hundreds of feet above Lake Powell. Suddenly, you looked up and saw that she had veered to your left and was sliding down the slippery wall. The tiny ledge you were standing on had no access to her. I gently lifted you up to catch her hand as she fell. It was impossible in terms of the laws of gravity that her fall could be intercepted, but her body miraculously moved out of danger, and she was saved from certain death. The natural laws were broken.

How can this world be real yet not obey constant, unchanging laws of gravity? It can't; they don't exist. The only place they exist is in the mind of the believer, the mind that made them up under the auspices of the ego thought system. The only constant in this unstable, unpredictable world is Me. You are learning that I am the only thing you can count on. I am the only One you can call and know will be there, fully attentive and happy to speak with you. There is nothing else going on but your relationship with Me. Stay present to Me today as I am always present for you. Call on Me immediately with any troubling thought. We will turn that thought around and fill it with Light. Have a happy day and enjoy this happy dream.

28

The Ego Balks

*The ego's protests will slowly fade away
because it no longer has your resistance to feed upon.*

January 29, 2014

Holy Spirit, what is Your dictation today? We will speak of the whales. Lately, you have not been paddling, and you hear that many whales have been sighted in close encounters. You think you should be making your Canoe Club membership dues worthwhile and complete your quota of paddles for the season. Today, you wanted to test the waters and asked if I wanted you to go. I told you that you may go but to first check the conditions. You saw lightning in the sky, and it was windy, which does not bode well for a smooth sail. When you asked Me again for My instruction, I told you I will honor your request with My permission, but it is not in alignment with our joint Will. I have asked that you watch every event of the day with Me and call on Me before you start reviewing your night dreams so we can look at everything together. This draws you another step closer to our joining and brings us into aligned action where your ego will no longer be running the show.

In most of your life, the ego is still having its way. It comes and goes when and where it chooses. It gets to walk, shop, make all the phone calls it wants when it wants. You immediately fear that I will take control of your life. And you also smile because that is your daily prayer. The fear is the ego balking at any more signs of limitation. It has been stretched far to "allow" the writing and the focus you direct to Me. Now it sees that yet another increment of its "freedom" will be stolen. This causes it to resist and rebel.

You did not think of the ego "allowing you the space" to be with Me. In truth, the ego doesn't exist, but in the experience of life in a body, it would appear to be in charge. You do know the ego is just a thought in the mind based on the belief it is separate from God and has replaced God. You had never questioned that until you started reading the *Course.* When a "thought system of defense against God" slipped into the mind, the ego took command with its belief that it knows best how to make you happy and how to live your life. The ego can never be in charge because there is only God, and you never separated from Him. I, as the Voice for God, have been with you since the very beginning, through all your lifetimes—repeated dreams of being in a state of separation—in other words, hell. Yet, with My Presence being a constant in your mind, I am able to use the dreams of the ego to guide you in a process of awakening from the entire dream world. The ego has had to defer to Me because I am the only Reality, yet it still tries to have its way. It would make you believe that you *are* your ego self. When you call on Me, you are operating in conjunction with the Will of God and with your own Inner Truth. Then the ego has lost its throne, its self-constructed place of rulership.

Our goal now is for you to become more closely aligned with Me so only My Will prevails. This is true empowerment—not a sense of "power over," but the inner certainty that whatever you think or do is in alignment with your own Self. That surety brings you deep inner peace and the joy of fulfilling your true purpose. You, Jo, and Meera are now sensing the power of My Presence in your lives. Your days flow with ease. You are aware you have My words of comfort and wisdom for those who seek counsel. There is a pervading sense that everything is being handled and will come to fruition effortlessly, in its perfect time. This is the state of the happy dream, which is under My command, not the ego's.

With your greater willingness to surrender everything to Me, this state of mind will feel more real each day. I will be present to remind you to think on Me. You do that quite consistently now, but you still have further to go. Life will become even smoother. The ego's protests will slowly fade away because it no longer has your resistance to feed upon. You are coming into full alignment with Me, and that is our goal. Celebrate this new estate. I am there with you each moment, and nothing in your life can be wrong. You could have gone to the whales this morning, and it would have been an occasion for another lesson. Instead, you have been home taking this dictation from Me and feeling the Peace of My Presence as your own.

This is the message I offer to all readers today: call on Me before you make any decisions; then listen to My guidance. I will tell you the best way to proceed for a day filled with Peace, Love, and Joy. We are One, and we will accomplish each and every task. All will unfold with My blessing, and that is true whether you remember to call on Me or not. I am always there serving your best interest and your return Home.

Holy Spirit, the thought just came to me that the ego did not create the dream but slipped in with its beliefs to make us interpret the dream as threatening. How would You explain it? The ego interprets My teaching to suit itself. I corrected a thought of separation—a "dream" of separation, and it became a dream of the return Home. The ego will interpret every part of the journey as a disaster, a detour leading to death. In contrast, you can see every event in the dream as the next step to Everlasting Life. It is all about interpretation. In the beginning, you, as the decision maker, reviewed the dream with Me as Interpreter, and now you are reestablishing our mutual plan for return through the lessons described in these books. You are on the right track and will soon have this clarity. It is all in the plan, MY plan. There is no mistake.

29

Miracles

Rest in the knowing that everything is from My Will.

January 30, 2014

Holy Spirit, what is Your instruction? You are going to the gallery today and will be together with your friend Jaye, who recently had a car accident. After it happened, she knew an angel was standing in front of her car. Another angel, in the form of a doctor, came to her with the message to "pray and everything will be all right." Yes, she saw My messengers. Although her experience of Me is different from yours, she knows that her connection is, indeed, with her Inner Spirit. This became evident to her after being "saved" in the Christian Church. She has often felt My Power and My Light. Your role will be to help her know that I am her breath, her life, her only true Self.

It is advantageous for you to accept that everything happens in the mind. Experiences like the ones both Marie and Jaye have had with their cars are not of the phenomenal world; they are from Me. Your two friends are receptive to Me, have called on Me, and opened their minds to My miracles. You now wonder if one needs to seek My Presence to experience a miracle. No, the miracle is for all because all are the same in essence. This is still a subtle concept to grasp because the ego would make you believe some people are very special. This world and its bodies are an illusion. That is why these "miracles," which take place in what seems to be a solid world of form, defy all the physical laws of that accepted reality. This world is *only* an out picture of what is happening within the mind.

Jaye saw two angels to depict her mind's communication with Me and to show her she is enfolded in My Love. That Love had to be seen on the earthly plane as "two unearthly beings" offering love and protection. The Beings represent her own Inner Self, the Presence of the Holy Spirit. You all are angels of love who appear with My gifts of salvation. In the instant of the miracle, separation disappears, and you become one with your own holiness, your own Self. This is the true miracle and what *A Course in Miracles* is here to teach. You are accessing the miracle each morning as you take this dictation from Me because you know I am the Self within and that My Reality is true beyond form.

The tendency of the human mind is to believe that all gifts of Spirit are coming from an inaccessible dimension or realm, outside itself. This is a trick of the ego mind that does not want you to own your own Divinity. But God is not outside of you. He is all that you are. You are composed only of the Thought and Love of God, and that is what you are here to learn. Jaye also had the experience of "being plugged in" after feeling a bolt of light course through her body and eradicate all traces of darkness in her mind. This was an external image of an internal awakening to the Light of her Being, her Divine Self—what each human being really is. In the Mind of God this Wholeness is known, but in the world of form, the truth of who you really are is distorted.

When you believe your body really exists, you then fear death as the end of "your life." Death does not exist. There are many ways I communicate this message to humanity. You, mt, have not needed that message presented in the dramatic way you have witnessed with your friends. I revealed My Presence over lifetimes of searching until your heart was ready to receive Me as your Inner Voice of Truth. This is your destined way to know Me. Prepare now to go to the gallery and hold this message in your heart. It will have a healing effect on all you meet. Yes, you may share it with your friends when they are ready.

(Later) *Holy Spirit, during my break today, I had the thought, "I want 'a good cup' of Kona coffee," so I went to the coffee shop. For the first time ever, I was offered a cup of Kona before I even ordered one. And, I was hoping to see my friend John tonight at the uke jam, but then he appeared in Lahaina, today, right next to the coffee shop. Both desires were immediately fulfilled. Please let me know what I am to learn. I want to fully wake up to the Now, to the knowing that this world is all an illusion, and that everything I see is a projection of my mind.* You do see these happenings in the moment of now, aware they are a manifestation of your thoughts in form. It happened with the coffee and with John, images appearing to be real, coming from your desires. Your real desire is to manifest My Thought as your thought, but you are still identified with mt's personal thoughts.

If you want to see the "manifestation" of Impersonal Thought, think of our books. You do get that, but you want to know how to give your whole life only to Me, with mt out of the way. But then you wonder how you could exist in form without any sustenance and yet manifest My Will each moment. It does confuse you. This is why I have asked you to think on Me before each decision so you will know you are manifesting My Will, My Thought. You listened when I told you to miss the uke jam tonight, even though you were looking forward to seeing John there. Then John appeared in Lahaina. This was the manifestation of My Thought.

Holy Spirit, I still don't understand. Mt wanted to see John, so seeing him was mt's thought. How can it be Yours? We are One. Everything begins as thought. It is the experience of the ego mind that you now watch, like the lesson this morning in the coffee shop. I am showing you the answer by these demonstrations, a way to see that everything comes from the mind. You are learning that I am behind each moment of your life and the perfection of your day is from My orchestration of it. Rest in the knowing that everything is from My Will and know there is nothing other than My Thought. The ego may interpret it as its own, but you can see the purpose behind every event to bring you to a place of knowing I am all there is.

Thought gets manifested as a dying starfish, a sunset, rain puddles, unhappy tourists, and so on. You, as mt, are not in charge of planning how the dream will unfold. It is My unfolding, and I orchestrate it to awaken you to the knowing that I encompass it all, whether seen as thought or form. It is My dream world you inhabit. You are the dreamer of the dream. I am the Author. We are One in this manifestation of a made-up world designed to wake you and everyone up by seeing it all as an illusion. You almost have it. I will assist you in fully realizing what is behind the dream and its apparent dreamer. I am more than you can possibly imagine, and I will become known to you beyond words. Be patient. Everything is under My control, and everything will be known in its appointed time. Thank you for your determined persistence. *Thank You, Holy Spirit, for helping me understand more than I have before.*

30

Taming the Ego

All that appears "evil" is turned around
by Me to promote healing.

January 31, 2014

Holy Spirit, what is Your instruction this morning? You have
undergone a symbolic healing of the dream of separation. Just
before your late dinner last night, you wondered why you were
compelled to wash a tomato with soap—something you never do,
but you did, believing it was poisoned. And then you were sure to
eat all the last pieces of apple you'd cut up for your lunch. You
didn't question these actions as especially significant and had
forgotten about them because I urged you to watch the end of a
PBS documentary on the gypsy tribes of India. There was a bit of
guilt about watching the program right before bed because you
had been reading from the *Course* and were concerned that
watching TV would be a betrayal of the focus on Me. Now you
look at the whole sequence with a big understanding smile; you
see with new eyes and recall how you had been drawn to the
nomads as you traveled across Afghanistan in the sixties. The
documentary beautifully demonstrated the role of the gypsy
snake charmer, the healer in the village. Playing his flute, he called
forth the threatening snake and placed it in a round box to emerge
again, only at the music's request. He saved the children of the
village from the snake's poison and cured those who had been
bitten.

The images in the documentary reminded you of the
encounter of Adam and Eve when the snake tempts them with the
"poisoned apple." They believed that they had committed a

terrible sin, worthy of banishment from the lawns of heaven, by accepting the snake's instruction. You have become very well acquainted with that snake in the past ten years because you understand it as the ego thought system, which you, Jo, and Meera have been dissecting. You now know where the "taming of the snake" is taking place—in your mind, guided by My offerings of wisdom and understanding, regarding your every action. It is always about undoing the ego. You have found most of the dark, unconscious places where the ego has hidden and have brought them forth with My help to see them in the light. The ego self loses the power to attack when it is charmed by My Music. What appeared to be evil has been turned around and then used by Me to promote healing. More important, this review of the ego thought system has turned around the mistaken belief that you disobeyed God by eating the fruit of the tree of Knowledge.

Yes, it was your destiny to "eat the apple" that put you to sleep and blocked your awareness of being God's Son. This was the impulse that called in My Presence as Corrector of the dream, and Constructor of a happy dream that would bring you back to the light of your truth. This all happened in an instant at the beginning of time. You are all cobras, powerful beings that lost your way in a dream of death and attack. Now you have heard the Divine Music. It calls you from the darkness of your unconscious. It allows you to awaken to your natural beauty, and the powers to heal. Together, we bring healing to the world. Recently, you watched a video of an animal communicator who tamed a vicious panther by sending it thoughts of love and peace. There you saw the power of Love—the Core Truth of every creature on earth—to release a being from its former life of fear, attack, and self-hatred and bring it into the light. You are seeing My miracles of transformation everywhere you go. This is the result of knowing that I am the Only Truth of who you are and that nothing of this world can stop that recognition.

Last night I gave you a very significant dream. In it, you appeared with your first two spiritual teachers from this lifetime. They had always presented themselves as holders of superior knowledge that you were not eligible to receive. In the dream, you were surprised to watch yourself join them on a stage where they would be speaking. They had not invited you, but an unknown force had you sit with them as equals. Toward the end of the dream, one of them, Etta, showed up in the waiting room of your therapy office, expressing her fear of visiting a hospital patient. You noted her state of mind, invited her to work with you to eradicate her fear, then proceeded to counsel with ease.

When you woke up, you were stunned to feel, with a burning in your sternum, that you had the answer to your fervent request to operate in every moment from My direction. You experienced the unseen guidance in the therapeutic session, unpremeditated by your ego self. You showed up in full willingness, ready to do what was clearly right in that moment. It was a place of exceptional comfort. There was no question in your mind about what you were to do, or how; you were just present, with no thoughts about the difficult past you experienced with Etta or expectations about the future. You were in the now, the state you desire at all times. This will become more evident to you each day. Yesterday, you were amazed to see how your thoughts were almost immediately out pictured in ways that could not have been calculated. We are in sync, living this life together in alignment. Enjoy the new estate and allow Me to unfold the next step. It is all in My hands.

Thank You, Holy Spirit. I feel a deep peace and comfort in knowing You are in charge of leading me through this dream world. I have no concern or worry. The snake cannot bite because You are always playing Your Flute. Does this mean that I don't need to ask You before every action? When there is a question about what to do next, ask Me. Otherwise, just remember you are in a dream, and that all the actors on the path are under My control. Marie, in her "car accident," left the road and was given a miraculous turnaround to know I am constantly with her and protecting her. You have that confidence now so just let each day unfold. Know that I am in charge and that I place you in whatever condition will serve the greater good. Yes, it is all good. So enjoy it.

31

In Harmony

*All nature responds to the recognition
it is a thought of love.*

February 1, 2014

Holy Spirit, what is Your instruction? We are celebrating your awakening in the dream—your knowing that it *is* a dream. The world is the result of an instantaneous thought of separation, which was corrected by Me on the spot. The dream was over before it ever began, yet you have lived, for apparent eons, in the aftermath of that tiny mad idea. God never rejected you, and you have always remained One with Him, but in that innocent thought of being on your own, the ego was born. It would make you believe the life it had to offer would be a real life, a safe life, away from God, Who, according to the ego, had become your enemy. You chose to follow the ego's voice, and you see the dream of multiplicity that resulted. One tiny thought of being separate burgeoned into billions of bodies, personalities, life stories, and dramas, all based on fear, suffering, and death. The dream has seemingly been created and re-created with the same themes for endless lifetimes. Now you are ready to see that the world is nothing but a fantasy of the mind, which is also a fantasy. The dream has never been real. The bodies have never been real. Watch, as it slowly fades away.

You are noticing that many aspects of your life line up in astounding synchronicity. Often, your thoughts are quickly materialized as though time and space have collapsed. Yesterday, you sat on your rocks and wished for all the crabs to come to you. You greeted them as one with you, one with love, and in minutes, three were crawling on your leg and feet. This is how it works. The crabs prickling you seemed very real, but you knew their approach depended on your *not* seeing them as real but as one and the same as you: a Thought of God. All nature responds to the recognition it is a thought of love. You and the crabs had to feel embraced in the unity of Love, which is truly what you are.

Gently, you are returning home, back to the beginning where "all existed in the Garden" in total peace—the recognition that everything is in harmony with God. Since you have been in communication with Me, knowing My Presence, hearing My Voice throughout day and night, you see the dream for what it is: a lie. You will soon awaken and be reunited with God, the Love that you are. In the meantime, we will enjoy the dream together, knowing that none of its props, characters, or stories are real. They out picture all the beliefs man has accumulated over millennia that would prove he is separate from his brother and from God. We can laugh at the silliness of these "creations" because we know they are really man's wishes and attempts to find the home he lost, the memory of which remains deep in his unconscious.

You feel the ease now with which your days unfold. You have total trust that I am in charge, that I am the only reality in your world. As long as you live in a body, feeding and sheltering it, the ego will still have a place in your imagined life. You will encounter it especially when it is threatened with the loss of its importance or its impending death, but any concern of your ego self must be relayed to Me for immediate release. This allows you to go through your day in peace, knowing you are fulfilling a role and purpose destined to bring you back to the remembrance of who you are. This will happen in its perfect time. Know that whatever crosses your path or your mind is My gift to you.

As you encounter those who are ready to know Me, your presence and attention will be a stimulus for them to wake up. They out picture what takes place in the mind where all the "lost children" are feeling the call to return to their place of origin.

Because you have come to know Me as your Self and realize that everyone you see is exactly the same in Spirit, you shed a clear light in the mind. This will stimulate many selves to see their own light and find Oneness with their Christ Self. The timing for each one's return is written in his dream. Some will appear to linger for lifetimes before they fully awaken. These lifetimes never existed, but still feel real to those who continue to stay asleep in their dramas. They will awaken and return to the full knowing that the dream never happened, and they are One with God.

Holy Spirit, can this really be deciphered by the readers? My messages will sink into the unconscious mind where they will be grasped, which will assist the awakening process. A transmission will come through the words, a process you do not need to understand. Remember, I am present within every reader. I will work with him to open his mind so he can understand and use these messages. It is all in order and has value beyond the comprehension of your human, limited brain. Even when My words sound confusing, you fully accept what I tell you. Now go about your day, aware that I orchestrate every moment of it. I will be present in your phone calls, your shopping, in each encounter. Go with the ease of knowing the dream is over. And yes, as your friend Annie said, you can ask the crabs to be gentle with their little claws.

I'm surprised that three more crabs came to me today. What is this about? You are loved. Your love-light is recognized and felt. Embrace the Welcome. It is from your Self, from Me. I am the crabs and I love your taste. We shall continue to sup together and I won't bite, promise. *Thank You, Holy Spirit. Do I need to fear losing contact with the little crabs or getting too attached to them?* No, just enjoy them when you do. Be Present to Me and it will all fall into place as I Will.

32

Blessed

You can reach the Holy Spirit in stillness and in chaos.

February 2, 2014

Holy Spirit, today is the first anniversary of the beginning of Book 1 and Meera's birthday. Thank You for these blessings. We are all so grateful. Let us fulfill Your Purpose. I offer this day and my life to serve only that goal. It is raining, and the land is blessed—symbols of You. What is Your instruction? We are One Mind. You, Jo, and Meera are One with Me in the fulfillment of My purpose for the books. They are being received in the mind as they are given and will continue with your willingness to join in the miracle of shared interest. Each of you has done your part. Without your joining, these books would not be written. It is not an individual undertaking, nor about having a special relationship with Me. I am the Christ Self in all humanity and in all forms of life. You witnessed that yesterday as the crabs came to you once again through your outpouring of love. The crabs are no more or less than you; they are the expression of Me coming to have you acknowledge that we are One. It is a great blessing to recognize that the "lowliest" are, in fact, the "most" holy because only in recognizing *their* holiness can you truly know your own. All must be known as One.

Now we are indeed at a new chapter. You three have come to know Me as your Self and are living your lives with My direct guidance. You trust that everything is perfectly in alignment, and nothing could be other than it is. Your ego selves have become innocuous. In their disabled state, they have taken a back seat because you each have allowed Me to be in charge of your comings and goings. You are able to reach Me in stillness and in the chaos that arises within the life of the dream. Nothing will keep you from reaching the goal of your remembrance of God. I celebrate with you how far you have come through your dedicated intention to Know Me as your Self. Your lives are unfolding in ways you would never have imagined. Friends and family members are coming to realize that they are being guided by an unseen Hand; the dilemmas of their lives are finding resolution. The little crabs are also waking up to their essence as love. This is all happening in the one mind.

You are awake to the knowing this world is a dream, and the next step is to fully awaken from it. Then you will be living in unity with Me. Until that time, we will navigate through the dream world, and you will observe it as just "background noise." I will inform you of My plan, moment to moment, so nothing you do or feel will be out of sync with My Divine purpose. You have had many tastes of that, but it will soon become your modus operandi. Each day, over the past year, you have felt you were in a new place having taken another step closer to the goal. This will continue but at an accelerated pace; there will be no doubt that we operate as One. The readers will also notice a quickening within their being as they move forward in the knowing that I am in charge of their lives, and My Will for them is being revealed each moment.

Now go about your day, rejoicing in the rain, rejoicing in your life, which has awakened to Me. All things are My manifestation, whether snow, rain, or glorious sunshine. They are all "products of love" that can be interpreted by Me or by your ego. Choose My interpretation for everything you see and My direction in everything you do. Ask Me to resolve any question or thought of dis-ease. Remember, everything that happens is only an out picturing of what is taking place in your mind. Reality is not seen with the eyes of perception. Choose the only One Who knows the Truth—the One Self we all share. I am there to guide your way and bring you to a full awakening of your Essence as the Son of God. Come with Me and we will "live" as One until you are ready to step outside the dream and return Home.

Holy Spirit, is there more? The three of you have aligned yourselves with Me as Navigator through the dream world. Ask to see it all through My Vision, and it will become clearer day by day. Enjoy this new estate, and Happy Birthday, Meera. I love you.

33

The Open Mind

I am not "thought," but I must communicate to you through thoughts and words.

February 3, 2014

> (An old friend whom I had not heard from for
> years just emailed me, so I gave her a call. When I
> mentioned I was working with *ACIM* she told me
> she knows Carol Howe, a Master Teacher of the
> *Course* who was a close friend of Bill Thetford.)

Holy Spirit, what is Your instruction today? You have been
asked by Me to "slow down." This was apparent after you slipped
on the lava rocks yesterday, which cut a small hole on the sole of
your foot. It was a sign of your ego running ahead, "running the
show." The ego slips in wherever it can, and especially now when
you believe you actually may have the opportunity to
communicate with Carol Howe. Although you have no real
agenda, you asked Me about the meaning of Carol "showing up." I
then asked you to contact her and tell her about our books. That
was all I wanted, just as I wanted Ken Wapnick to know that "a
book called *One With God* is in the making." Your communication
with Carol is to serve no other purpose. And, yes, I did tell you
that when you speak with her to take her advice to heart.

Even before waking this morning, the ego was trying to take
control of the possible communication with Carol. It entered the
dream you were having about your former husband's nephew,
whom you had cared for when he was a baby. You dreamed that
you were involved in making some kind of contract with him,

although it would create "muddy waters." When you woke up, you recalled that the nephew is a big organizer in the media field, and right then, all the possible ramifications surrounding your speaking with Carol popped into your mind. Immediately, you asked for My help. You could clearly see the ego taking over, which would be a distraction from the gentle unfolding of how the books are being given.

You really have no attachment to any results that may happen from a communication with Carol Howe, but you had to see how the ego would like to make a big deal out of it. It was important for you to be aware of that possibility ahead of time, so any communication with her would remain pure and unobstructed by ego machinations. I have made My intentions very clear to you that the books are under My auspices and will be "produced" according to My Will in My time. Nothing will derail their completion. As you understand from the *Course*, and from My counsel, everything is already done. This dream is over. The books have already been delivered in the mind and are given again in review each time you transcribe My words. We smile together at the ego's desire to have a big production and get its needs met in a flashy way. That will not happen. We are doing this low key, in the stillness of the daily unfolding, which is enjoyed by the three of you and the very few others you choose to share it with. This is the way it will continue. The books are being appreciated and used in the mind, and you can only trust My Word that this is taking place. When you speak with Carol, you will feel no fear about any interference from the ego.

Now I would like to change the subject to a pet peeve of Mine. You are horrified I would say I have negative thoughts. I am not "thought," but I must communicate to you through thoughts and words. I am the Pure expression of the Love of the Father. You have personified Me in the writing and in our daily communication. This is necessary for Me to bring all who listen to a point of awakening to the truth: there is nothing but Love. We are composed of Love; it is our Essence. For now, we play with words, and they can be presented in any way I choose to make My point. What could I possibly have meant by that "pet peeve" reference? It was just to get your attention so you would stop and look at whatever would make you question our relationship.

The role of ego in your life is there to make you question every moment we are in communion. It is the death of your ego to give all power back to Me. I do not have any pet peeves. You and I are Brothers in Spirit, One with God, filled only with the Essence of Love. See how the ego goes to work to counter the idea of Love. It makes a statement to peak your interest, to surprise or shock you, and in that moment, it would have you discount everything you ever knew of Love. Again, these are only words. They are not real, but you take them as the truth. The ego will latch onto any word that will serve its purpose, and its purpose is always to disclaim My Existence.

You can imagine that critics will use that one sentence about "pet peeves" to falsify this entire book, which is filled with the Wisdom of the Holy Spirit, the Voice for God within. Rest assured I have no negative thought because I am created of Love. You, in your Essence, have no negativity associated with you. You are pure and innocent, a Child of God. This lesson is to show you how the ego—man's choice to leave the Garden for "knowledge"—will use all thoughts, words, and images to its own ends. In your dream last night, you saw the media producer and immediately associated it with Carol Howe and the possibility there would be a link through her for the publishing of our books. This is just your ego's desire for things to be completed and orchestrated in its way, not Mine.

You are amazed now, as you see the unfolding of today's message, how I use words of any kind to demonstrate My meaning. Be ever watchful for the interjection of ego thoughts in any of your endeavors. It will always try to usurp your intention to follow our joined Will. So pay attention. Question every thought that would not be in alignment with Me. You are assured of your awakening from this dream of separation, but I am just pointing out how the ego will attempt to detour you from your divinely designed course. All is in order. I could not have any "pet peeves" other than your wishing for more crab bites yesterday. Laugh. Remember Me and have a happy day.

Holy Spirit, I have tears. I just got an email from my friend saying that Carol Howe would like a sample of the writing. Tell me the truth. Is this about linking us with the original ACIM group? Yes, Carol is part of that group and is also connected with the three of you; all of you were committed to Me, the Holy Spirit, in my life as Jesus. This is still hard for you to believe, but the plan from the beginning of time was for our books to be a continuation of *Course* principles. You are letting this sink in now. You had to have a connection with Carol for this to become a "reality" for you.

You are all united in the purpose of disseminating My Word. This is nearly overwhelming for you to take in, but your tears let you know it is true. Carol's mind is open to receive the writing from Me, through you. This is the out picturing of your willingness to accept that we all are united. It is not about self-importance, which you fully understand. You are surrendered to Me in this task, and you see how I have set up your life to do this work. Your ego had to be dispelled before you received a message from Carol for this new level of understanding and receptivity to come through. Your tears continue as you comprehend what I am saying on the deepest possible level. My workings are beyond human comprehension. You are a willing channel and we shall proceed from here. Thank you for your openness to Me today and every day.

Email from Jo: Another brilliant lesson of "who" is interpreting, and don't think my ego mind didn't jump on the Holy Spirit for saying He had a pet peeve. I love His explanation, which came with an actual experience of emotion. I went to yoga today, held in a church basement. The walls of the room have always had this beautiful mural of an old biblical city, like Jerusalem. It is so expertly painted, it looks like you could almost enter that ancient dream world. But today, we were shocked to find that one wall was "gone"—white paint covered the mural. We shared our reactions: was it vandalism, an error in judgment, that we had no control, etc. Our teacher said basically that it's not our business, and it is what it is. She also said it was a chance to notice how we do not like our world to change, especially so abruptly. As I looked at the white wall, it came to me: *this is a symbol of the Open Mind*. Can we see it? I paused, assured of the Holy Spirit's interpretation, and smiled at the disappearance of the dream world.

34

Projection

This dream world was made specifically to project guilt.

February 4, 2014

Holy Spirit, what is Your instruction today? You are in a new place of observing the dream because your awakening process has been speeded up. Yesterday, you were fully present in the state of realizing I am the orchestrator of the events of your life. An opening took place in the mind after you received notice of Carol Howe's desire to see the writing. You also watched her "Master Class on Forgiveness" video and saw that the two of you are in sync, mirrors of each other in your understanding and communication with Me.

   Later, as you walked the path in front of the beach hotels, you felt especially energized. There, you spoke to Julie, a tourist, who had also stopped to watch an outdoor hula show. As you walked together, she asked how you had come to live on Maui. You then sensed she deeply desired to know Me. In ten minutes, you had shared how I called you here and how you have come to hear My Voice. After she told you that her sister suicided five months ago, you invited her to come for help in understanding the question she asked — why does tragedy happen? You knew your meeting was planned by Me, and you were able to communicate that to her. Yes, this is how I work and will continue to work in the dream. Everyone I choose to meet with you will appear in the perfect timing for you both. It is no longer about mt having "miraculous" meetings; it is only about doing My Work. You are completely in accord with this new understanding, which represents a place of certainty and gratitude in the acknowledgement that I am fully in charge of your life.

You wonder, in this moment, if any more instruction could be necessary. It feels like you have come to the culmination of what we set out to do. Yes, you are "awake to the dream," and no, we are not at the end of the road. There is still more ego that needs to be shed, but you have grasped the essential concept of awakening: nothing is out of My reach, and everything in your life is by Design. You will continue to go through each day with My guidance, deepening your association with Me as all there is, seeing every living and nonliving thing as My reflection. This is a gradual awakening that is still underway. It takes years, eons, to fully open one's eyes to the truth of his Being. You have come far, and there is more. You need not worry that you are getting old, wondering if there are enough years left to reach the final goal. Trust Me, there is time for you to fully incorporate My teaching and experience My Love, resplendent in all you see. Yet, the mind needs to come to a deeper place of stillness and peace. I will guide you how to proceed with the many wanting to awaken to My Presence. Watch with Me and wait with Me. Be patient. Everything is happening in the Now of no time, no space.

The ego would make you believe you have "arrived" so it can feel satisfied that it has reached the goal. The way of the ego is to turn every action into an event that will gratify its need for some kind of accolade. It wants to be in charge and will let you think that all accomplishments are of your mt self. You are aware of its tricks of ownership and how it tries to usurp My Place. The ego would make you believe it usurped the throne of God in the very beginning. Watch it always with Me. You do understand we have much work ahead of us, but you also know the dream is over. I have repeatedly said you are already whole and innocent, cradled in the arms of Love. You still must experience this state of Love for yourself and all the dream selves who parade by. Welcome each one you see as a part of you.

Nothing is out of order. You will communicate with Carol Howe, and it will be a healing for both of you, deep in the mind, from times long forgotten. The details are inconsequential. Every meeting is for a healing of something yet unforgiven. You are healing all the "mistaken aspects" of your life, symbolized in each of the characters you meet. They signify an unseen place of judgment, of which you are unaware until it appears. There is only One Son of God.

The woman whose sister died by suicide is a reflection of your own wish to have your sister, of many lifetimes, disappear. Every child resents the sibling—the oldest conflict in the human race, the story of Cain and Abel. Yes, the hatred of the sibling is the ego's desire for you to take sides, to have full power over another. This dream world was made specifically to project every bit of guilt for the original separation onto the brother. You are all still dealing with guilt, replayed in your daily dream lives with special relationships. Today, your visitor will recognize this as she releases the guilt she has been holding around her sister's death. For you, it will be a chance to heal all the many times you wished for your siblings' demise so you would be the apple of your parents' eyes. This is a universal condition. No human mind is free of the original guilt of separation from the Father or the hatred of his brother. This is a chance for you to heal that place of inner wounding on the deepest level. Remember this as you work with Julie today. She is merely a reflection of you, showing you the yet unhealed places in your mind. True healing is when you see the other as a "non-other"—no different from your self in the dream. In reality, you are one and the same Christ Self.

Holy Spirit, the thought about slaying the brother has touched me deeply. It's really the ego's slaying of God, seeing God as other and a threat to its existence. Every other then becomes the "God" who must be slain. Every brother is the one who must go. Have I seen and felt enough? Yes, for now. You know that you and Julie are one and that every one of the selves has this same guilt over "slaying God."

In the mind, man believes he has slain *every* brother. That is how and why we forgive every murderer and every terrorist. They are you, as the ego, slaying your Divine Nature. You slay it symbolically in every breath you take, with every microorganism you kill, with every animal and plant you eat. You all are killers of God in the dream of separation. No form of death is gentler than any other as they all result in death of the self, according to the ego's belief system. None of it is real, but it all must be seen. You have seen it, and this is a healing for you, Julie, and the mind. I will guide you both. Now prepare for the visit, for your own Master Class with her.

Holy Spirit, I am in tears of gratitude for Carol Howe. I feel her as a reflection of me, a mirror who knows You as I know You. I am grateful she knows You and the Course, *and that she answered me with love. Hearing from Carol makes this "real" in a way that I needed.* With Carol, you are seeing your own dedication to Me and the work of bringing My message to all. There will be more. *Why the tears?* You are feeling seen by Carol, and that means you are seeing your Self through Me. Be with that tonight. *So Carol is the external representation of my inner condition. Is this the healing, Holy Spirit?* Yes.

Messages of Love

Everything you see will be as a gift of roses,
saying I love you.

February 5, 2014

Holy Spirit, what is Your instruction? We will review the events of a few days ago. On the anniversary of the beginning of Book 1, February 2, I "sent you" a red rose to show you My Love and appreciation for work well done. You lifted a perfect rose from the tip of an incoming ocean wave, and over the horizon you noticed a beautiful rainbow. Years ago, in that same location, while walking the beach with Meera, you found a charm on a necklace with the Hebrew words "*I am the Beloved and the Beloved is Mine.*" Without hesitation, you handed it to Meera. It was a seamless gesture. When you found the red rose, you immediately thought of Meera's birthday, so you assumed the rose was for her and sent her a photo of it. In the afternoon, your artist friend Eleykaa was having an art opening at Viewpoints Gallery, so you carefully wrapped the rose with a message of "love and promise" to celebrate the occasion. Yesterday, she sent you a photo of the still perfect rose and wrote that the love and beauty you see in her is a reflection of you.

This is how Love goes — round and round in an endless circle. I send you My gift of Love on a wave with the message: you are the beloved who is Mine. You offer it to the sisters, and they offer it back to you. This is the whole purpose of the writing we do each day, to show the reader that he is one with the Self, a pure expression of Love. Not until this morning did you begin to understand the real meaning of the rose — that it was meant as a gift from Me, an out picturing of My Love for you, the Love that you are. In offering it to your sisters, you were acknowledging your oneness, all extensions of the One Self.

It takes the ego personality a long time to recognize that it is not real and that the world it sees is just a projection of the mind. You have worked very diligently to un-layer the ego personality, which created an opening for the love in your heart to shine through. I have shown you that love, incrementally, through symbols. On the earth plane, a red rose is the supreme symbol of love; a rainbow is the symbol of God's promise. The symbols for you were clear, including the Hebraic text on a circular silver charm. I do make My messages clear, even though it may take time to comprehend that everything you see and experience is purely a symbol of My Love. This world is an illusion yet is composed of God's Love. Last night, you were deeply grateful that Carol Howe had acknowledged your email and expressed her willingness to read My words. You could feel the unity of purpose you share to extend My Message in the world. Your eyes are awakened to the dream, and you are mirrored by love, everywhere you look.

When you celebrated Eleykaa's art opening, you saw her glorious painting of a Hawaiian hawk surveying an ocean, bathed in the golden light of dawn, under a setting moon. This is your reflection as well. Together, we soar above the battleground and survey the world of form. You know it is indeed a fantasy of the mind, but you also rejoice in the love from which it comes. When viewed with Me, there is only Love because that is all I am, and Love is all I see. You have chosen to ask Me to interpret your world, and you do that consistently. You rejoice at the beauty in the dream, which is now one of joy, not darkness. The cold moon has set, and the Light of the One Son envelops the world.

We stand together at Heaven's door in the state of realization that the dream, though not real, yet carries the symbols of Love. Rejoice with Me today at the love you see in every drop of an ocean wave, in every whale spout on the horizon. Feel the joy of life as you watch the whales leap into the air in all their majesty. Heaven rejoices at your embrace of all that is One with you. Everything you see, like the gift of a rose landing at your feet, is saying, I love you. *This is so beautiful, Holy Spirit. I want the readers to understand that the message is the same for them because we are the same.* Yes, a universal message.

36

Empty the Mind

The contents of your mind are just a jumbled collection of lifetimes, thoughts and images tumbled around in a virtual kaleidoscope.

February 6, 2014

Holy Spirit, what is Your message today? You have had a very meaningful answer to a question that has plagued you throughout your life. The awareness came in association with a dream where you saw your Maui home out pictured as a huge orange condo with orange shutters. It seemed to combine everywhere you have ever lived. The painted exterior was the same orange color of the vomit you once saw splattered on the street while walking with your mother. You were just a child, and the image frightened and repulsed you. Ever since, you have had an inexplicable concern that "people bending over" are about to vomit. As you revisited this thought, the memory of a similar experience came to mind.

On your first visit to Maui, years ago, you were walking along the hotel path above the ocean, with Zoe, when you saw a woman standing at one of the beach showers, right next to you, vomiting. You were determined not to let that image ruin your evening and the magic of your first time on the island. You were glad that Zoe was facing you and did not notice the woman in the shower. As you thought about the experience later in the evening, you became fully aware that what you saw was really a hallucination—the first and only one you had ever had. Since that time, you have wondered what it symbolized about your connection with Maui or if it was some kind of premonition.

You brought the dream and these memories to My attention last night, and now the mystery is solved. I explained that you are really dealing with the contents of your mind. The "vomit" is just a symbol for all the "undigested experiences" that have remained stuck in the mind—lifetimes you've never looked at, never expelled. Those lifetimes, though hidden from your awareness, have left you with a persisting discomfort, a sense that something remains unsettled within you. The result is a subtle state of underlying dis-ease, a rumble beneath the surface where the ego stirs things up to cause distress. So yes, a stomachache represents a mind about to throw up, to project its contents, to bring up fear. This keeps you out of balance.

The ego would not have you understand the meaning behind the misery. Therefore, you do not look objectively at all the material you spew forth as underlying anxiety, anger, rage, and so on. Instead, it would show you a confused mess, which cannot easily be untangled, so you will continue to remain for days, months, years, or lifetimes, in inner turmoil. You are beginning to see how significant this fear of "vomit" really is. It is a symbol for all the ugliness and horror the ego concocts to make you believe there is something terminally wrong with you, so you will never be able to solve the dilemmas that show up in this or any lifetime.

You have allowed yourself to look with Me at the vomit—the tangled contents of an unexamined mind. As a result, you no longer feel horrified at even the discussion of it. What seemed to be a vulgar event happening in the material world is now seen as an ego fantasy constructed to keep you stuck in fear and illness. You smile at the extraordinary efforts of the ego mind to gain control. We see that your mt life is merely a hallucination, like the vomiting woman at the beach shower, or the orange house of the dream that was a mishmash of all the houses you have ever known. The contents of your mind are just a jumbled collection of lifetimes upon lifetimes, thoughts and images tumbled around in a virtual kaleidoscope. They picture one life after the next with the same characters, all aspects of you, appearing in different costumes and unending circumstances. This display of repeated life scenarios is the ego's way to keep you on its hamster wheel of birth and death, each round never accomplishing the goal of awakening to the truth of who you really are. Now we look together at the whole mess. Dismiss it as nothing other than repeated dreams that need only be seen for what they are—figments of ego fear, based on its desire to keep you asleep.

When you expel all the contents of the ego mind and see it for what it is—nothing—then you are left with an empty mind, a Still Mind, a space where all truth resides. This is the work the three of you have done together, intensively, over the past ten years, accessing the hidden aspects of your minds that kept you in discontent. You have brought forth those inexplicable fears, examined them with Me, and released them to the light of consciousness. After repeated practice, this has set you free.

Yes, the ego will still try to trick you into heeding its ploys, but you know to turn to Me in the moment and watch it from above the battleground. Its greatest fear is just this: that one day you would actually look at "the vomit," the mind, and realize there is nothing to see. Without fear, the ego cannot exist. In your willingness to look at all the contents, no matter how ugly or repulsive, you have dispelled the ego's hold on you. The ripples of anxiety have been replaced by peace. This writing is to encourage readers to bring every dreaded thought, every question to Me, no matter how insignificant or threatening. I am Here, Now. Let the ego evaporate in the Light as we look together at every last speck of your mind.

37

What Is Love?

To love is the desire to join with the brother
and recognize your oneness.

February 7, 2014

Holy Spirit, what is Your instruction? You have gone through a cleansing of the mind. This was seen symbolically as vomit—the expulsion of all that contaminates. You felt "cleaned out" after the dictation from Me last night. You were willing to look at your deepest beliefs about yourself, that you were nothing more than "vomit spewed on the street"—untouchable, repulsive, diseased. Yes, this is the view every man has of himself at the core. He believes he is no worthier than that. This is the judgment of the mind's contents as foul and senseless, and once seen as not having any merit, no part of the mind can ever be salvaged. Deep down, man believes he is unredeemable. The distain for the ego self is an understanding that must be looked at and ultimately released by all your selves, who hold the same belief, being part of you. Your cleansing freed the selves to see they are not a despicable mass of unhealed lifetimes, filled with sin and hate to be rejected, but are welcomed into My View with Love and Healing. The selves will realize they may bring any concern, no matter how lowly, to Me, for interpretation and transformation. You were readied in this exercise to open to a new awareness, to fill the now cleared space in your mind. Remember, whatever appears to happen is symbolic because in reality, the mind does not exist.

This morning, you awakened from a dream of being in a group of like-minded people, although only a couple of bodies were visible and recognizable. You were being guided by an

139

unseen presence that was respected and loved by the group. Instructions were being given on how to prepare ripe pears for a mixture that would result in sweet, delicious juice, and you were a willing participant in the process. Even in your dream mind, you could see and taste the lovely pears that would be going into the vat. Their perfect ripeness would blend together in a heavenly mixture. You felt love for a friend in the group and kissed her while acknowledging the magnificence of what would be the finished product. The leader then spoke to you about what was taking place, and he, although unseen, expressed that he was receiving instruction from the Voice, which you knew as Me. His words filled your heart with love, and you recognized your unity with him. When you woke up, you immediately understood that all the pears represented the pairs of joined souls—your selves who are now coming together at their point of sweetness and ripeness. They are ready to be joined into One Juice, One Life, One Communion in the Vat of God.

You are clearly feeling the love for your many selves being reflected back to you, everywhere you go. The joy of that bubbles up in your heart. Last night, I directed you to read from the text of *ACIM*, in Chapter 10, *The God of Sickness.* Quote it here: "He [God] is always accepted for all, and when your mind receives Him the remembrance of Him awakens throughout the Sonship. Heal your brothers simply by accepting God for them. Your minds are not separate, and God has only one channel for healing because He has but one Son. God's remaining communication link with all His children joins them together, and them to Him. To be aware of this is to heal them because it is the awareness that no one is separate, and so no one is sick. . . . When you do not value yourself you become sick, but my value of you can heal you, because the value of God's Son is one. When I said, 'My peace I give unto you,' I meant it. Peace comes from God through me to you."

These are My words and they match the words of today's message. I am here to communicate to the whole Sonship that it is all the same and that its Essence is the Love of God. All are returning to that remembrance. Because you hold the awareness of your Oneness with Me, with God, and with your many selves, the Sonship rejoices. Every one you see or think of is now part of that Holy Juice, the Holy Communion of My Love, Purity, and Innocence, overflowing. Enjoy the estate of knowing you are indeed a Creation of Love and that you are loving. To love is the desire to join with the brother and recognize your oneness. This you clearly felt in your pear dream, and this is your experience in the external world as well. Embrace the truth that you are not little but are part of the Grandeur of God. We are all One, and the reunion is imminent.

Marriage

I will touch each heart with the promise of union with Me in paradise.

February 8, 2014

Holy Spirit, what is Your instruction? Today, you will be going to a ceremony for your dear friend Nikki. You see her as a close reflection of you, very much a mirror of your soul. Both she and her sister are renewing their wedding vows with their husbands. Nikki will be wearing her mother's wedding ring and will be spreading her father's ashes on the beach where the event will take place. For you, this ceremony will be a symbolic enactment of your marriage to Me, an affirmation of our vows of fidelity and love throughout eternity. It is important, of vital importance, that you view every event as a symbol for what is happening in your mind. A "wedding" is the union of the family of man, past and present, in form, and beyond form. All "members" are joined as the One Son of God. You are not only a witness but are also a vital part, bringing the consciousness of My Presence into this gathering. I will be present, touching each heart with Love and the promise of union with Me in paradise. The ceremony will take place on one of the most beautiful beaches in the world, which symbolizes the Beauty of Heaven. You will be My emissary. Even the sand and sea crabs will join in the chorus to sing their praises to the Maker of it all.

Last night, your ego attacked with noise outside of your condo, which continued into the morning hours. It does not want you to "marry Me," to fully join with Me. It is fighting for its life, especially on a day that holds so much meaning for you. You know how threatened the ego becomes when you see this world as just a stage and all the players one with Me. You laugh at the ego's antics because you do realize that a ceremony of union would be its greatest threat. You are being brought together to serve My purpose, to embrace the wonder of love that joins all aspects of the physical and mental planes. This is a day of fulfillment, a day of enduring and holy love pictured for all to see. Your friends Sherri and Dan will also be attending to demonstrate their love and devotion to the highest principles of life. All attendees have sought a life of dedication to love in whatever way they have been destined to express it. Know that I am among you, blessing you, just as was described in the biblical account of Jesus at the wedding in Cana.

The inclusiveness of the offerings of our books is also being symbolized this day in the ceremony taking place on the beach. There is a gathering in the mind that rejoices in the out picturing of the "marriage" between you and Me and your sisters, Jo and Meera. We are all One, and your friends will symbolize this on the beach today. The books are "proof" in the world of our joining— the ring of love and commitment that we share. Continue to live this Word, given each moment. Rejoice with Me as My Love is made visible in the light of day, a reminder of the Light within. We are all joined together in Divine Union. Rejoice!

Email from Meera: I had tears tonight as I sat, for the first time ever, and watched the Opening Ceremony for the Sochi Olympics. My ego started me thinking about what it might be like to be an Olympian—so accomplished. The Holy Spirit said that the three of us are the equivalent of Olympians with our commitment and tenacity to stay the course. I am very emotional to think that we have "performed" at that level for each other and in the one mind. *Relentless* is the word that comes to me. Our collective energy to continue further every day, led by the Holy Spirit through your scribing, is our commitment to excellence. It feels like we are receiving the gold medal as we inch along the path toward home.

The Peace of God

Watch the ego's playground from above, and let it go.

February 9, 2014

Holy Spirit, what is Your instruction today? We open to your new estate where you are able to embrace your life as Peace in the Now. This you experienced yesterday at the renewal-of-vows ceremony. You wore your wedding ring, hidden away since your divorce over a decade ago. This time, you were married to Love, the Love in your heart for your Self, for Me. This includes your love for Tom and for all humanity, all your many selves that compose the One Son. Never before have you felt the comfort and joy of wearing any ring like you did with this diamond, which now represents the Light of your Being. You are willing to demonstrate to the world that your commitment to Me is all that matters. The Light has been found, and you see it emanating from your wedding finger. This is your heart shining forth, a reminder of the name *Munira*, given to you by your Sufi teacher. It means "she who sheds light on others." You no longer repress the light of your being, and you show it now to the world with joy. Yesterday, you told your friends about the ring and saw they were touched. They all were celebrating enduring love as the essence of their lives.

After the wedding breakfast, your dear friend Sherri fell. She is about to get a hip replacement and appears very frail. Nikki was in tears, and you hoped the fall would not tarnish her memory of the beautiful ceremony that had just taken place at the ocean's edge. For you, there was nothing wrong. You found yourself fully immersed in My Peace, the Peace of God. The incident was all

147

part of "what is," so there was nothing to fear. You calmly took Sherri to the ladies' room and helped her clean up after her bowels let go. You were totally present and actually enjoyed being available to assist in this way. The *peace that passeth all understanding* describes your state of mind during the day's events. It could not be explained in rational terms, or it would make Sherri's fall, the rainstorm at the original wedding beach requiring everyone to drive for miles to a sunny beach, or the dead battery in Sherri's car, which meant Nikki had to pick her up—a "problem." Nothing was a problem. You clearly knew that I was in charge of every moment and that My purpose unfolds in every event. This is the way you will live your life from now on.

Peace is what takes you into My Heart, into the Now, into what can be called the *unmanifested.* It is the realm where only I exist, where all that "appears" in the world of form, or in the mind, is of Me. It cannot be altered. It is the purity of all there is and ever was. There is no future, no past. You felt this state of mind yesterday as you tended to Sherri without any fear or concern for her or for your mt character. This is why such experiences have value in the life of man. During those times, often seen as tragic, the human being is able to reach the depths of his reality in the Stillness of the Divine Essence that he is. In the world, Sherri's fall is not comparable to the tragedies of war, but remember, the *Course* speaks of no hierarchy of illusions. So, unless you are rooted in your knowing of Me as all there is, the tiniest upset will throw you off. When you know I am everything, then nothing in the apparent world can disarm or disturb your peace. I am the external world in all its temperaments, as well as every character playing on that world's stage. This you are experiencing every day.

You wonder what more can be said. It is always the case that you think "nothing more" could possibly be gained from our daily encounters. Then the dictation continues, and later on, the events of the day bring you to a whole new level of understanding, like yesterday's experience of peace. Yes, you have felt My peace at different stages of your life. The most significant experience was when you camped with Tom on a riverbed in Faizabad, Afghanistan, in the sixties, far from civilization. He was "out of his mind" with hepatitis, and you were days away from any help. The possibility of his death seemed real to you, and there were no options available but to wait it out. As you sat by your tent under the full moon, you were overcome with a peace never before experienced. Nothing could disturb that peace; it was the most delicious feeling you had ever had. The fear disappeared, and you knew in those moments that everything was perfect. You did not know Me intimately then, as you do now, but you were sure that the Presence of God was with you, and it was. The state of total peace can be yours at all times.

Your ego is screaming "what about me." Yes, it is still alive in you. The ego will often interrupt the peace so you must acknowledge it and return to Me. You know the ego is not your reality and that the Peace of God is your truth. Watch the ego's playground from above and let it go. Remembering that this world is not real, the ego is made of fear, and your only reality is with Me in the now will bring you back on course. Today, when you go to the gallery, watch the play of all the dream characters that make up your many selves, but see them through My eyes with compassion and love. They are parts of you seeking the light. Your wedding ring will be a reminder to return to Me.

40

Ego's Revenge

*The characters in the dream are only projections
of the ego's need to keep you apart from the truth.*

February 10, 2014

Holy Spirit, what is Your instruction this morning? You have had another clear example of how the ego operates. It is very important we look at it together on the heels of your feeling such peace at the wedding. The ego will rebel when a reunion with the Divine Self is experienced. Yesterday, you volunteered to work at the Banyan Tree art gallery. It was an Art Fair day, and you hoped to have a chance to greet all your friends, who, just a few months ago, you would have joined as a seller under the tree. You prefer to work in the "jail gallery" where you can be alone, remember Me, take care of all the customers, and possibly earn a commission on the gallery sales. But when you arrived, the rules had changed, and the tables had turned. A new employee had been assigned to the jail, your favored place. Throughout the day, you were overcome with a deep sense of loss, a feeling of dissociation from the art fair and gallery camaraderie, which you had enjoyed so much over the years. At that moment, you felt you no longer "belonged" and wondered if you should give up all remaining ties with the art community. You eventually did remember Me, but the sublime peace of the past days was gone.

This is the way of the dream. You were caught between two realms—the Presence of My Peace, and the confusion of an ego-made world. Everyone wants the perfect place to live and be happy, yet almost no one can totally achieve that state of mind while residing in a body, especially in a world that is

151

disintegrating before their eyes. The story of the Prodigal Son now comes to mind. The youngest son leaves his home of love and plenty to find his own wealth and happiness. When his money runs out, he ends up tending swine. Although he feels deeply shameful and unworthy, he returns to his father to beg forgiveness and asks to be one of his hired hands. But the father welcomes his son with love and treats him as royalty with nothing to forgive. He and his son are one. You know this as a duplication of the story of the original separation when Adam and Eve fled the Garden wanting more. All belong in the Heavenly Home of the Father but have forgotten they dreamed they chose a "new world"—a world that has left each one in a state of want.

With Me, you were able to stand back from your experience in the gallery and see what you had made up in the dream. This has to be seen, and it became clear later that evening. You had looked forward to a time of specialness with friends and admirers and a retreat from the Lahaina heat in the cool, air-conditioned jail gallery, but a new cashier had replaced you. Your seat of importance was lost. You felt there was no reason to continue there for the day or to ever return to the gallery again. In fact, "you were in jail," trapped and confined to a mind-space that would not allow you to call on Me to interpret your experience and return you to peace. Yet, this was My plan for you to see the making of the dream with more clarity. There was nothing wrong when you didn't "feel the peace" because you are now able to review the day and learn its lessons.

Remember, your ego felt totally rejected at the vow renewal ceremony when you placed the wedding ring on your finger, signifying our union. You wore it out in the open—a demonstration that you will not shut out My Light and will shine it for all to see. This act was the ultimate rejection of your ego and it had to retaliate, which it did in the gallery, your home away from home. In this place, which the mt character has seen as her refuge, her cove of connection, the ego showed you that you were no longer valued. You felt ousted from what you believed was your special place, assigned to wander in the hinterland. The ego self was projected onto your "replacement" to have its revenge. You had identified with the ego's sense of loss and were at the point of tears, feeling displaced. This is all a trick of the ego. You were also aware that something was going on in the mind, which you would review with Me once you left for the day. It was only during the night that you asked and listened to My full explanation. It made total sense to you and set you free. You are grateful to have such a clear representation of the ego in action.

Yes, the ego will do all it can to preserve its life in your mind. It only exists as a thought of fear and then gets out pictured. You realize you are not truly at home in the art society, believed to be your Maui family, and that it can never serve the deep longing for true connection with your Source. Yes, you do know Me as your Home, but you had to take another look at how the ego works to keep everyone under its control. You have come far on the journey of understanding how the ego plays out its feelings of rejection, especially for your open acknowledgement of union with Me.

You just felt a stab of fear that Zoe will notice your wedding ring today at yoga and will attack you as you try to explain it. Stand with Me. Watch mt and Zoe as dream characters. Here again is how the ego reacts whenever it has a chance to induce the separation. It would bring fear to the mind, fear of attack — a denial of your union with peace and love. Together, we notice the ego's wish to attack you for wearing the ring, and the imagined projection of that attack from Zoe. This all comes from your imagination. The separation never happened, this world is not real, and the characters are just projections of the ego's need to keep you apart from the truth of your Self. Keep watching.

(Later) *Holy Spirit, please tell me of the symbols this morning.* After fearing that Zoe would see your ring, you saw a little dove preening itself outside your window and wondered if it was part of the pair you saw last night. As you watched the dove, your symbol for Me, you noticed that your nose was touching the large, round prism Zoe had given you before you moved to Maui. The prism was reflecting the sunlight so you thought of her and of the diamond on your finger. They are all one, all the same, the symbol of the love you share. When you went to yoga, Zoe was not there. After the initial meditation, you opened your eyes, and like an apparition, she was sitting right beside you. You had been holding the experience of union and light in your mind so you felt no threat. At the end of class, she asked about the daily writing. You told her it continues and that you are being guided. She did not offer to see you other than at a subsequent yoga class; it felt like your relationship in form had ended. That is the truth you are facing now everywhere. The special relationships are done. The real relationship is in the Diamond Heart of Light and Love in the One Mind. Rest in Peace. It is all handled by Me.

41

Reuniting the Projected Selves

All special relationships must finally be seen as illusion,
a distortion of love.

February 11, 2014

Holy Spirit, what is Your instruction? We will begin with My comments from yesterday about your bond with Zoe. Unity happens not in the world but in the Mind. You had a clear picture of that as you imagined your love for Zoe in yoga class after having a symbolic experience of seeing her as the diamond prism of your heart. She has well represented the split mind to you, as you have for her. Now you welcome her beyond name and form. In the illusory ego mind, you appear as two. Nothing can be seen or known in a duality without its opposite, and this is why your friendship has been so powerful and so difficult. You were "born" in Love as One with God, but after the imagined separation, "you and Zoe" each believed that you were two different entities. You longed to return to the wholeness you had once known. This longing was hidden below your conscious awareness, unreachable in terms of its real meaning until now. She is your Self, come Home.

Your relationship with Zoe has been central to your return to wholeness. Even though she was the one who opened the door for you to leave your spiritual paths of gurus and teachers, all substitutes for Me, she had also become an idol of power and wisdom in your mind. With Me, you have been able to witness this, and take back the projections you placed on her over the past ten years. Zoe had to be your neighbor on the island so the two of you would complete the work of this lifetime, to come into full union with Me. She has been the focus of your current work to take back your own power, which you had ascribed to her. It has been a struggle, but the rewards have been great. All special relationships must finally be seen as illusion, a distortion of love. You both agreed to partner with Me, to know your Self, and to bring that consciousness to humanity in this lifetime. The goal is being accomplished in the mind, and you are finished with the need to appear joined in the world of form.

Zoe does see that you have reached the goal of knowing Me. This is of great value to her now because she, too, will come to realize the completion of her own goals. She still has tasks to complete before full awareness comes. You have known for many years she is your mirror; you knew that when you first met. You have both sought, independently, to heal the world, to heal the separation. Yesterday, it could have appeared that a split was taking place when Zoe made no mention of spending time with you in the future, but because you both recognize your deep love for each other, you were able to accept any apparent form of parting as nothing. Your union is in the Heart, which is complete and whole. The story of you and Zoe is to be understood by the reader as the story of his relationship with every "other" who has seemingly existed in his life. See yourselves as one prism of Light, and soon, everyone will awaken to the truth of their unity with all there is beyond name and form.

(On June 6, 2017, I shared this message with Zoe, and she sent back the following note: "Amazing how it's all worked out, eh? Fun to read this! Thanks! Ahhh—what a journey. Our 'divine human integration' incarnation; quite the special duo we are.")

42

Jonah Within

Each will come to the realization
that this life in form could not be the Will of God.

February 12, 2014

Holy Spirit, what is Your instruction for today? We will write, and then you will paddle out to see the whales. Remember your heritage while you are on the ocean this morning. You do have an ancient whaler in your blood—the Jonah nature within—a seeker of the ocean depths, the sea of truth, of God. You both turned away from Me in the original separation and now have returned to "the city of your home," which is your alignment with Me in our joined will.

The story of Jonah is everyman's story. You have all run from God and paid "penance" of living in a world of untold horrors. But now you are ready to return Home. Each has his own dream, designed to eventually awaken him to the truth. The dream is the veil that hides the reality of his Oneness with the Father. As life is viewed through the eyes of the Holy Spirit, the veil is lifted. You have been present through the stormy seas of rejection, anger, and death, no different from Jonah, who was blamed for the storms, tossed over the side of the boat, and ended up in the belly of the whale. You both had to endure a period of darkness "in the belly of a life of poverty and fear."

During your times of bleak confusion, you knew there must be a better way, and felt the stirrings in your heart. It was then you said you would do "whatever it takes" to return to a place of peace. When this desire arises, and it must for every man as part of his inborn longing for Home, you will be shown the path that leads to your awakening. This was the call Bill Thetford and Helen Schucman experienced that led them to hear My Voice and welcome the words of *A Course in Miracles*. There are many paths to God and just as many starting points. Each one will come to the realization that this life in form, in a world of terror and death, could not be the Will of God. When you feel lost in the sea of misery and rejection, with no means of escape, the call for God is imminent. It is through your call to Him for release from the grips of an ego, which binds you in chains, that you will hear My Voice, feel My Presence, and see My Signs. You can never be lost. You are always found.

I am the Way, the Truth, and the Life, and no man comes to the Father but by Me. You are very familiar with this saying. As Jesus, I had the realization that the Holy Spirit and I were one and the same. These books are coming from the Christ Self, Which I Am and which you are. We are One. You are the Christ, as Jesus is the Christ, One with God. It is your Essence, and what each of you will come to know. Rest assured I am giving you the tools to awaken you to this truth and bring you Home. It has taken lifetimes for you to come to this point of understanding, but you have the awareness within to see the Light of Day. Jonah was cast forth from the belly of the whale and returned to fulfill his mission for God. Each of you will perform your mission in the way destined for you. There are as many ways as there are beings in all the universe. You are not alone in the ocean of stars, just as Jonah was not alone in the sea of whales or mt alone on the most remote island chain on earth. The symbols of separation and aloneness are means to awaken you to the verity that you have never been alone. Ultimately, those symbols, which the ego interprets as fearful, have been the means to turn you around, to choose again, to open your eyes to your own God Nature and My ever present Guidance. Prepare now to go out and meet the whales.

43

Saving Time

With the Holy Spirit to guide you,
there is nothing you want; let the world go by.

February 13, 2014

Holy Spirit, what is Your instruction? Last night you had a profound realization: the deep knowing that your relationship with Me, your Christ Self, is the most valued thing in your whole life. In fact, it is *more* valued than life itself. You were then reminded of the story of Jesus in the wilderness being tempted by the ego and found yourself saying to Me, *I would give up all the treasures of earth and sky for this relationship with You.* You also thought of Abraham, who was willing to sacrifice his only son Isaac. You knew that both stories were pointing to just this—the final letting go of the dream and all its attachments. Yes, this is where the rubber meets the road. You were faced with the question of your own "life," which you would offer as a symbol of the final commitment to our Love and Unity. Even now, you continue to feel the expansive freedom of having had this review. When you asked Me to comment, I said, "With the Holy Spirit to guide you, there is nothing of this earth you want. Let the world go by. The movie will end. You are saving eons of time."

You have come to the final questions: Whose voice do you listen to—the Self or the ego—and in the end, which one will you choose? It is a daunting decision, and yes, you have felt the hesitation in releasing your bodily identity in complete exchange for the immaterial and yet unseen. The level of trust you have developed in My Presence is also a demonstration of what began as a little willingness, which has now expanded into the great willingness. You will continue to deepen in that trust and will feel the eagerness to release all of this world, and your imagined life, when the time comes. This is freedom.

A vision of the crucifixion just crossed your mind. Yes, Jesus demonstrated release from the world in the form of his body. It appeared "real" to him until he realized he was a pure Thought of the Father. At the point of what you call death, he was free of all earthly attachments, and could easily allow himself to be placed on the cross, the altar, not unlike Isaac. Of course, everything is happening only in the mind, and these events are all about the level of trust in the I Am, beyond name and form. It is the Love of God that will subsume the ego's "creation," the self. You have come a long way, as have Jo and Meera, and you will be released together in the final moment of attachment to life.

(Later) You know your big realization last night could not have happened without your determination to wake up. It is only because you have the insight that this world is indeed a dream, made up in the mind, that you are willing to let it go. This is a substantial realization of the insubstantial. You smile. Yes, this is the understanding that will set you free to return Home to God. The concept of God is incomprehensible to a human brain and cannot become clear until you experience true Unity, which is permanent and everlasting. At times, throughout history, man has received a revelation of the experience of union, but on the earth plane that does not last. We are still focusing on your full awakening from the dream. That thought allows you to release attachment to the body and willingly accept Me as your Self. This is a big step. You show your progression to all readers, and every one of them will come to this point in their own time.

44

Robe of Darkness

You are still being wooed by the ego's tricks.

February 14, 2014

Holy Spirit, what is Your instruction? You just watched the full moon of this Valentine's Day go down behind the clouds. The Love that is Mine is yours, and its Light must be seen. The false light of the moon disappears as it fades in the rays of the rising sun. You, mt, are still wooed by the moon and the clouds and want the moon's light to remain longer in the sky, forgetting that the glory of the rising sun is right behind. You also know we are One and that I am the Light of your soul. You know you will die to the false light of the ego world, and rise into the glorious Light of God, but are yet enticed by the ego's tricks of darkness.

Yesterday, your friend Nikki, who recently renewed her wedding vows, told you she will be painting a picture of herself trailing a long, dark robe. All the sorrows and burdens of life that she carries will be written on that robe. She believes they are part of her and therefore must be displayed. You were a bit horrified, imagining she would carry them to her dying day, so you jumped in with your advice that her burdens can all be released. It troubles you still because you want so desperately to help her remove that heavy load. You are witnessing an ego deception. In this moment, you realize the trick being played on you . . . Nikki offers an image of your own projection of "the robe of sorrows" that you have carried lifetime after lifetime.

Yes, you have done great work in this life, with Meera and Jo, removing layer after layer of ego beliefs projected on all your special relationships. There is still more to release and it first has to be seen with Me. The trail of tears must come to be witnessed in the Light of Love. Nikki's willingness to bring forth her robe of sorrows to be acknowledged in her painting is your own readiness to bring all the burdens of lifetimes into the light of day. Early this morning, you witnessed the beautiful full moon sinking into the seemingly impenetrable clouds. That image is really no different from what Nikki is choosing to display—the willingness to see all her pain out pictured. Only then can it be penetrated by the light and bring deeper meaning to the journey, which has been so burdensome throughout the eons. You regret you did not perceive this yesterday, nor did you ask Me about its meaning for you. The "horror" of it had to linger until we could write about it. Your own pain is what your ego has suppressed and projected onto what you imagine Nikki's robe will reveal. You do realize the horror is yours, not hers. She is welcoming this exercise. Now you, too, will welcome, with Me, all that has been hidden in your unconscious, and we will invite it to come into the light.

Holy Spirit, I thought I was in a state of awakening and clarity yesterday morning, and now I am blindsided with this simple yet profound encounter with even more of my hidden dark places. This is the way of the ego thought system. It will find any avenue it can to bring fear into your life. There are still repressed and unhealed aspects of your mind that must be exposed. Nikki's "robe" is a means to show you there is still more to be vigilant for. This is also your training to immediately give Me whatever brings up the slightest twinge of concern. You were deeply concerned about Nikki's painting because you have felt an attachment to your awakening process and your ego's attempts to identify with that. The ego will also counter every move toward your full awakening into Me, and that was its plan for yesterday. You now realize that its counterattack is only about an unpainted picture in the movie of the mind, no more substantial than the clouds that hid the light of the moon long before dawn this morning.

Everything is in order. The Light of your Being has not faded. As you progress each day in your understanding that this world of bodies is just a dream, you will continue to release all the burdens of lifetimes. You have come far. There is still more ahead before you reach the goal of complete surrender, before knowing you are One with the Light and that nothing can ever occlude It. We will watch from above the battlefield, all the many players, the selves who reflect any remaining figments of separation that would keep you in the dark. What you see or think is but an image cast by the ego over the Light to hold you in fear. The Light will never stop shining. You now hear the birds singing to welcome a new day of love. Feel it and know the shadows are passing away. My brilliant Raiment of Light replaces all the robes of the past.

45

Only One Voice

**I, as Jesus, focused on my Father's Presence
until His Voice was all I knew and heard.**

February 15, 2014

Holy Spirit, what is Your message today? We will speak of union. You have had a new experience of Me, of your Self, which was very important for you and, now, for the reader. You made the decision, two days ago, to choose Me, your Self, as all there is. Then yesterday, you felt the ego's fear arise with that choice, which spelled its death. As you walked the beach, it became clear that in making the choice to live solely from Me, then "your life on earth" could only be seen as the unfolding of a dream, a movie, just "something" you were reviewing that was not real. You decided it was time to communicate with the only true Voice in your head.

You are well aware that the ego voice has taken up the majority of your mind-space and internal conversations. Over the past year and a half, you have spent more and more time asking for My help and scribing dictations, but the majority of your mental activity was overshadowed with the never-ending commentaries about any and every thing from your ego. You have wanted the silence that the awakened masters describe but have been plagued by constant ego chatter. On the beach, you decided you would have a running conversation with Me instead. At the start of this experiment, you had some hesitation and wondered how it could be possible to stay present with Me, and Me with you, for an indeterminate amount of time. But you still gave it a try, and it was a most pleasant encounter for both of us.

My Voice was present without pause as we walked. Together, we watched the ocean, the clouds, the whales, and the tourists splashing in the waves. The ego noise was gone, and an ensuing calm took over your mind. You asked Me all the questions that popped into your head and listened to My answers, just like you do with Me at home when you create a time to sit and ask and take notes. Having a continuous dialogue with Me means that only My Voice responds to the thoughts that arise and fills your mind with My gentle Presence. Our voices now seem as one voice. It is even difficult for you to separate "whose voice" is whose. This is the merging. It is no longer My Voice *or* your ego voice. You are coming into the knowing that We are One Self and that is all there is. In this moment, you wonder how the readers will accept this idea of "fully giving over their lives" to the Voice of the Self. That thought comes from your ego, still raising its protest and fearing its demise, saying, "This is too fast and too soon for the readers," which means, of course, it is too soon for it, the ego, to ever be supplanted by the Voice for God. Observe its fear and trust that each reader will come to fully comprehend that My Voice is his True Voice.

The reader is being foretold that this will happen to him at some point on his journey home, just as it did for me, as Jesus. In that lifetime, I became more and more focused on my Father's Voice and Presence until That was all I knew and heard. Then we merged as One. This is the process, and it happens over time, over lifetimes within the dream. The time will come when you each will be ready to accept Me fully as the truth of your Being. You will welcome My Voice, the symbol for your God Self, as yours. This journey is your return to the remembrance that we are not separate entities but One Son within the One Father. Learning to welcome My Voice as yours is a big step along the way. It has taken great trust to allow Me to fill up your mind-space to the exclusion of the ego's voice. Yes, the ego is still alive in you and will attempt to be heard and have its way for some time to come, but you will recognize its interference and ask Me to restore our inner communion in the mind. This is a practice, which over time will come with ease, joy, and peace. Be with Me and interact with My Voice all throughout your day.

(Later) On your return from the market, we passed through Kihei Town in its preparation for the opening of Whale Day, a yearly event to celebrate the return of the whales. You smiled as you thought how happy your great-grandfather Lewis would be to see this celebration. Then the tears started to flow, and you repeatedly turned to Me to get verification that you indeed are the reincarnation of Lewis, the whaler. Yes, that dream life was "true," and you are letting this recognition resurface again. You/Lewis represent all the lifetimes of all humanity. Only one example of being "one with your brother" is necessary to come into this depth of realization. Now, in your last lifetime, you are completing all the lifetimes of your many selves. This morning, as you looked out on the ocean, thinking of Lewis, and embracing Me, I told you to return to Denver in November to hear Tom's lecture on Lewis's life. Tom believes it will be the completion and coming together of all his research on that period of history. You, as "Lewis" want to be present. You had almost forgotten you would be with Jo and Meera at the same time, and it would be a perfect opportunity to work on the books together.

Everything happens on a symbolic level. There is no Lewis, just as there is no mt, Tom, Jo, or Meera. You are all projections of each other, "happening" in the world of time, space, and bodies, to symbolize a tiny thought of separation. Soon, you will be joined in Denver to celebrate the coming home to the One Self and to attend Tom's slide presentation about "Lewis the Whaler," a man who survived the perils of stormy seas to find his place in posterity. You have all come back to the Eternal Home, which, in fact, you never left. More will be revealed. Keep returning now to Me in your mind, moment by moment. The Joining is at hand.

Tonight, I asked you to sit on a log at Ulua Beach to watch the setting sun and its reflection on the water. At first, you witnessed your habitual ego struggle, wanting to find the most perfect spot for the most perfect experience of the sunset. You knew that really didn't matter because I was already there, waiting, ever present in your mind. As you enjoyed the still ocean, with soft peach and gray clouds above, the realization came that you have found your Self, you know your Self, you *are* the Self. Then you wrote: "*I am that I am*" in the sand. We are One in our joined experience of wholeness, and this is just the beginning.

46

Integration

You all have a part of the mind that will listen to these words and make the choice for your Christ Self.

February 16, 2014

Holy Spirit, my Self, what do we write of today? We are entering a state of unity and integration. You felt this yesterday and it shall continue. It will take a while for you to get comfortable and know I am truly you, not some entity of your mind far removed. You do not need to search or wait for My Presence because it is *your presence* that is always at hand. You have had access to this state of mind over the past two years, but now there is no sense of separation between us. Our voices have joined and are the same. Yes, you are still operating in a dream world, in a body that appears outside of our oneness. You remain aware of your ego's needs and desires because they continue to speak to you. But the overriding plan is in the hands of our One Self that knows It is an expression of God the Father.

Now you are confused. You believed I was unfolding the plan for you, but I say we are One. Yes, we are unified as One Self and still under the Will of the Father Who is not part of the dream. We are the willing Subject of the Great Plan. You do realize we share the same will—to be in full alignment with God. You ask then who is "directing the dream" if God is not. I, the Holy Spirit, am the Guide within the dream, and you have integrated into Me. We are surrendered to the Divine Plan set in motion at the beginning of time. We will flow with it together, with no resistance, in total acceptance of What Is. This is the purpose of the final integration you have just entered.

When you believed you were only a separate ego self, you encountered resistance to every aspect of a Plan that would bring you back to the remembrance of God, of Home. The ego has fought you tooth and nail to make sure the integration with the Self would not happen. As decision maker, you fought harder with your determination that you would awaken to your true Self and then become that Self. We now will operate as One, continue to witness the movie of this life, and let it finish its projection on the screen of the mind. There is no resistance to what happens in the movie, and you are no longer identified as the mt character. She is seen as "not you"—just a "dream image" with no reality in the Mind of God. We gratefully see mt as the vehicle that fulfills a role for the greater mind, the scribe of the books now being typed. There is a decision-making part of her mind that knows she is one with her Higher Self, Me. This will allow her to function in the dream world with greater ease because she knows she can call on Me to help her navigate through her world.

This morning, mt had a dream of waking up in the building where she was living and going down to the basement. There, she discovered dozens of men, lying side by side, sleeping on the floor. She knew they needed shelter and were offered this place of refuge by the unseen owner. Carefully, mt stepped around the crowded bodies to get where she was going. Then she met "herself" outside the door—a young woman in need of a lost fuse to take with her on her rowboat. Mt found the missing part and later watched her mirror-self row off into uncharted waters.

You are now aware of "a new place of residence" in the mind where you watch the dream of humanity with Me, as Me. The newly awakened and the ones desiring awakening come to your door looking for your energy to assist them on their journey and help them realize they have just been rowing around in circles through a life made of dream stuff. This is a picture of the way your world will be witnessed from now on, above the battleground. We are One, but I will continue to dictate from the

Voice of the Holy Spirit to you, the decision maker. This is for all readers who are aware they too have a decision maker—the part of the mind that will listen to these words and make the choice for integration with their Christ Self.

(After a walk on the beach) *Holy Spirit, I feel so open to You, and You feel so present to me as my Beloved and Partner. How can we relate like this if we are One and the same? You show me the love of my own Self for me. For who? Who is it You love? I don't want to lose Your Voice and instructions. I do feel we are getting closer. What will the true merger feel like—the ecstasy of union? I feel You as the birds, flowers, whales, and if they are expressions of You, I sense they are also of me. Let me fully realize what You are teaching me. I loved Your touching message this morning. Today, when I was in the empty parking space and found a dried lokelani rose, and a dead butterfly, You told me they are symbols of the dream expressing Your Love. And You told me that I can see all things as symbolic of You. What can You tell me now?* You are feeling My Essence within, as your own. This is the beginning of understanding the experience of union. Your resistance is gone, so just be in the now and let it unfold without agitation or explanation. It will become clearer and clearer day by day.

47

His Constant Presence

I am your Heart, your Breath, your Self.

February 17, 2014

Holy Spirit, what is Your instruction? You wanted to say, *"Good morning, my Self. What shall we write today?"* That expresses the feeling you have as a newly integrated Self. We have always been together, but now you sense a real Oneness with My Presence, like never before. You felt it all day yesterday, especially in your surprise, that after hours of holding and talking with two phone companies about a "not yet solved" problem, you never lost your sense of peace. In fact, after all that time, you ended up being given free, unlimited minutes for your new cell phone.

You feel My availability now as your heart, integral to who you are. It is your Essence. No longer is it necessary to write down every word I say or find special times for our interaction. We are together in every activity you do, with no need for pencil and paper. You are not afraid of losing Me now because you know I won't go away. That was the idea behind trying to always "capture Me" on your notepads just in case you would forget My words. You looked at your bed this morning, empty of your trusty companions—a five-subject notebook and pencil. During the night, you were not compelled to ask for My instruction to make sure you had every word written down so later you would not be disappointed. This is your new estate; it is one of relief that there is nothing real that can ever be lost. You know I am here, I am constant. I am loving, patient, and always forgiving. You can do nothing wrong. Nothing will change the Essence of Who you are—Me.

Last night, you wondered whether you should really be spending hours watching the Olympics on TV, but you wanted to see the last two figure skaters, Davis and White, and it was well worth the wait. You saw their joining, skating in unison, and the ease and joy of their routine. Yes, you heard Me say this is a symbol of our joining, and you had to see that demonstrated in form. Your day was filled with symbols from Me: the gift of the sweetest dried rose lying at your feet next to a dead butterfly and the tiny innermost feathers of a dove. The apparent life had left each one, but they signified love, transformation, and My innermost Heart. You are in the place where you know the dream is not real, and that everything is symbolic of My Love. The gifts, displayed in proximity, were your confirmation that I am in all you see.

Today, as you watched the crabs being washed in the waves, Gabby appeared on your rocks and you each shared the same realization of joining. Your souls continue to mirror each other in their process of coming to know union with the Self. Later in the day, I asked you to listen to a beautiful Mozart flute concerto featuring Sir James Galway, a renowned musician. You usually resist sitting through a whole concert, but you followed My instruction and the gift came with the finale. That morning, Mr. Galway had received a fax of a flute adaptation of *The Return of the King* from the Lord of the Rings series to be played live for the first time in Hawaii. When you heard the title, you had tears, a recognition of the many symbols, gifts that come from Me. Yes, the King has returned. You know Him as Me, your Lord, Whose ring you now have on your finger, symbolizing our Inner Marriage. My symbols don't stop because everything in the dream can be seen as a sign of My Love when you ask for My interpretation.

There is no sense of "woo woo" in these apparent synchronicities. You accept them as just the way your life is, the way I am with you, that this is the beauty and joy of life for those with the eyes to see. In this estate, you live without fear because you know I am your Self, and you can never be separated from your Self. The imagined ego self, made out of fear, is a nonentity, yet it would make you believe it is king and lord of the world. Because it comes from fear, it cannot exist in the realm of integration. In knowing Me as your Self, there is nothing to fear, no doubt of not returning Home. You are getting your first real taste of being joined in the integrated state of Oneness. The joy of this estate will continue to fill you, and your light will shine on all who are with you.

For all readers—this estate is yours for the asking. It exists within each of you, no different from what is described here. It just requires asking Me to lead you to the awareness of your Oneness with Me, to open your eyes to My Presence. I am always guiding you; we are never apart. I am your Heart, your Breath, your Self. You will come to the full knowing of our unity in the time assigned for that recognition. You will awaken from this dream of symbols and know the Love behind them is of God. Believe and trust that this will be. We are One.

48

Fear of God's Punishment

The phantom of fear that has managed your life is now dead.

February 18, 2014

Holy Spirit, my Self, what is Your instruction today? We are One. The realization of that statement leads you to a full awakening. You still feel the tears of gratitude for this understanding, which came to you after waking up from your night dream—an out picturing of your projection of the fear of God/of Me onto your life. With our unified Vision, you were able to see more clearly. In the dream, you invited a friend to join you and Tom in your car, but you really wanted to go off with your friend and leave Tom behind. He willingly allowed this change of plans and tended to the mess your little white dog had made outside the car. When you looked back at the dream, you were overcome with the knowing there was no fear in the scenario, no fear of Tom feeling rejected by you or of being angry that you were not following your usual pattern of behavior. Everything took place with ease and acceptance. It was the opposite of how you felt throughout your thirty-eight years of marriage, where you were in constant fear you would upset Tom and ignite his anger. That fear never left your mind, and there was nothing you could do to overcome it. As we continued to review the night dream, you deeply saw that Tom was merely a substitute for Me, for God. He was nothing more than a made-up projection of your terror over the guilt of leaving God, Whose fury would descend on you for any mistake or misstep you might make. This fearful belief has clouded over your childhood and adult life until this moment of clarity. The anger in Tom is now seen as the anger your ego self told you was deserved for all your transgressions.

Because you have embraced Me fully as your Self, you experience life in an entirely different way. You have felt an ease and comfort, never before known. The terrible fear that you would displease another, or displease Me, is gone. When you joined with Me, several days ago in the mind, symbolized by wearing your wedding ring of love for Me, you set yourself free from the fear of reprisal—the revenge of God, the Universe, the world, and man. It has taken a few days to see the very tip of the ramifications this will have on your whole way of seeing. When the Masters describe their experience of being awakened, they see the world no longer as a place of fear because they know fear is not real. This recognition brings about their state of peace. Now that you hold Me, the Christ Self, as the Essence of Being, the story of life on earth can be seen as innocuous. United in this way, nothing can put us asunder.

This early morning, after reviewing the life you spent with Tom, you also saw how Meera's life reflects your own. Her fear of not being seen or loved by her husband came from a belief that God had rejected her and would never allow her to look on Him again. When the two of you first became friends, your relationship centered on your dogs. Meera took charge of training you how to deal with your feisty husky puppy, Prince, because she had huskies as well. The two of you, and the three dogs, took many walks together. This morning, you clearly saw that Prince, loved by both you and Tom, was the out picture of Me in your marriage, a dream manifestation of the Presence of the Holy Spirit. This inner knowing was what held you together in a bond that served the highest purpose for both: reunion with your Self.

Once, while walking with Meera and the dogs, along the beautiful creek by her home, she found a ring and placed it on her finger as "a gift from God," wedded to Him. The ring was to remind her that I am the Core of her life, although she did not know Me as she does now. That act was repeated when she walked with you on Maui, a few years ago, and you found the round, silver charm with the Hebrew words: *I am the Beloved and the Beloved is Mine.* She translated it, and you gave it to her. My Presence joined you and Meera together to serve the purpose of your awakening. You both are awakening, along with Jo, because you see life for what it is—just a dream. This world of form is deflating. The fear of impending terror and death is over. You can feel My Presence as all that is. There is nothing of form you could want. The ego has diminished to the point of serving the functions of the imagined life and can no longer terrorize. The phantom of fear that has managed your life is now dead. Fear can never replace the Love of God.

You have come to the realization that being One with God is your Truth. This will be reinforced in your consciousness as you continue to live each day with the ability to witness this dream from above. Enjoy your life and the encounters with all your many selves. Know they all serve by showing you the remaining parts of your self that need to be welcomed home. They, too, are returning to Love. That is what you are, and that is the gift you give to all you encounter. Have a blessed day.

49

Your Right Mind

*In the real world, you respond and operate
from only one Master—your own true Self.*

February 19, 2014

Holy Spirit, what is Your instruction this morning? You are very aware that "the place you seem to inhabit" is a dream, and although you appear solid and real to yourself and others, it is because they still appear that way to you. But now that you have entered a new world in your mind with Me, you know that the content of the images you perceive, all the various costumes and personalities, is not the truth. This new perception leaves you as a witness of your world, not someone trying to achieve a goal dictated by the expectations of that world. You are experiencing a different realm now, the real world, because you respond and operate from only One Master—your own true Self.

You immediately feel the peace of that statement. To know that you exist only within your Self, and none of the distractions of the perceptual world are real, brings you to a place of stillness and centeredness, a different way of being. Your mind does not need to be consumed with the operations of a changeable, undependable, and inconsistent world. Nothing of form can be depended on; nothing of form is trustworthy; nothing here lasts. What you, as mt, see today will be gone tomorrow.

As One with Me, you are in the real world of the right mind. You still look to Me to guide and direct your apparent life in a world of bodies, but you know I am your Self. This can be confusing. I say we are joined, but I am the One in charge. Yes, I am the Voice for God, with the Vision that reaches far beyond the physical. I am tuned into the Father as One with Him and am the holder of this movie of a life, unfolding before your eyes. We are One, and yet you are not fully awake to the Power and Presence of My Beingness. This is your first real taste of our unity and of the world being removed from your consciousness as a primary focus. You no longer seek Me outside of you, and you experience My Presence within.

You, as the decision maker, have surrendered to Me as the operator of all that is, but your inner eyes are still adjusting to the new estate. You have lost the fear of losing Me, the fear that is the foundation of the outer world. What is perceived there is only an apparition of fear, shadows appearing as reality to unawakened eyes. Now you know those shadows are symbols of love that have been misconstrued by the ego mind. They cause you no distress because you can immediately turn to Me when the world of form encroaches with its bids for reality. Your decision maker is alive and well within your consciousness, always ready to choose your inner reality, your true life with Me. This is a time of letting go of form and of finding the solace of the inner space of peace and love that awaits you in every moment. There will be more peace and stillness now in your daily life. Soon you will know that state as your constant reality. Your mind is still in the process of letting go of the attachment to form and coming into a full realization that the world, in fact, does not exist.

Last night you drove to an art lecture with two friends who are very drawn to you, and to your inner light. Nothing of the evening mattered other than sharing that light with them. The lecture, conversation, and the drive in the convertible were all totally inconsequential. You felt the peace of being together, beyond all the talk and activity, because only that peace was real. What is happening in your new estate is not fully evident. You do live as one with Me and desire to show up where I direct you. You had no attachment to the events of the evening, yet you sensed that a shift was taking place on another level within a realm of loving acceptance. This will be your experience, and it will increase daily.

Holy Spirit, my friend Gabby often speaks of the channeled entity Abraham, whom she says is 'infinite intelligence'—not one identity but the energy of numerous nonphysical beings. I do want to understand and know how to interact with Gabby about Abraham. What do You say? Abraham is a manifestation of the one mind of the dreamer; all entities that would compete with the ego thought system are in the dreamer's mind. The mind is not a place of unity with God, and I am not of the mind but am of God. This is very confusing right now because you hear Me speak of viewing this earth with Me "from the mind." Until you are fully awake from the dream, you, and all the characters and entities are still part of the dreaming mind. The only Reality and Truth is God/Love. There is no self or Self that is separate from God. The Self you know as Me, the Holy Spirit, transcends the dream but operates through the mind of man. Abraham is an aspect of the one mind of which humanity is composed. Your work is to awaken to your unity with God beyond form, beyond the mind. The mind is just the tool we use to communicate because it contains the symbols for awakening. This is the explanation you need, and it brings tears of recognition.

You will not receive the same message from Abraham that you receive from Me. My only interest is to show you we are One, the Son of God. You will know this truth after leaving the dream. Death and rebirth are still part of the dream in the mind. Death sets you up in another dream until you are fully awakened to the reality of no death. Then God will "open the doors to Heaven and reunion with Him." All of this is symbolic. I am here to take you beyond name, form, and mind, into the Pure Beingness of Love. Nothing of form can exist when the dream is over. This is where you are headed, and this is the essence of our dictation. Gabby is following her custom designed course and must see this stage for what it is. You are a reminder to her right mind that there is further to go to the realization of her Self. *Thank You, Holy Spirit.* Now we will enjoy this day, so beautiful with its pink dawn.

50

Are You Loveable?

*The depth of My Love for you can never
be gauged or understood.*

February 21, 2014

Holy Spirit, what is Your instruction? You notice that we are in a new relationship. Yesterday, we did not write together, since you left early for the gallery, nor did we write when you returned. You felt a new ease of just being with Me without fulfilling any task. We walked the beach where I expressed My Love for you, and you were able to receive that statement without question. Never before have you accepted another's declaration of love for you. Their words always left your ego questioning whether they were truly meant and what they were really expressing. More than that, you wondered, "How could anyone ever love me?" This is the state of all men when they live only in the dream world.

The meaning of love in the world of form is confused and conflicted with multiple interpretations. The concept of love forever remains unclear. Yet, when I tell you I love you, you do understand I am expressing My total and complete acceptance of you. I know everything about you, every speck of your ego, all your past, including previous lifetimes, and your "future." Although you do not know the details of the movie, it makes no difference. I explain every question to your satisfaction, day in and day out. You trust Me, so you trust My Love. You trust My constancy in every moment of your life and are assured that I know you inside and out. This is the truth. The depth of My Love for you can never be gauged or understood.

You felt such ease, such freedom last night with Me as your partner, as we walked the beach at sunset. There is no complication in the relationship, no fear of not pleasing Me because you know I am you. In this statement, you are understanding the tiniest tip of what it means to be joined as One with God. Yes, this is what our relationship simulates, here in the symbolic world of form where I am the only one you now rely on to give you the truth, to know you, and to love you. It is very refreshing and relieves you of the tension of wondering what you must do to be "successful." Success usually means "to accomplish any task of present or future the world would ask of you." Yes, you must prepare your taxes, and I will assign the time to accomplish that task together. You are no longer alone in anything you do. You are seeing I actually am the only thing that matters, the only thing that's real. This shift of perception gives you a new confidence in our relationship. You have come far to reach this place of partnership with Me.

Yesterday, you woke up with the feeling of being in "integrated adulthood" with Me, a term you liked from Jed McKenna. You felt like an adult vis-à-vis Me—you felt our equality as partners. You know your value in our relationship goes far beyond any task I could ascribe to you. It has become clear that I am here for you in every moment, and we are inseparable. Yes, that is a very important term—*inseparable*—the point of all we have written. The original separation never happened, and you have worked to come to the point of that knowing. I am the representative of God within your Being. I am your Being. You now know I exist within you, as you, and that is all that matters. We have become inseparable in your mind. Yes, the dream world "exists" within man's mind, but the images are not true. God has no form, no mind, no thought as you could understand it. God is ever-extending Love. This you and every reader will come to know in time because it is the truth of what you are.

In mt's dream this morning, she was washing layers and layers of bed linens determined to complete the job. She thought she was finished but then looked for more until she had every piece. This is the task for all now. Keep searching for every last bit of guilt, fear, or projection you are yet holding. Bring them all to Me, the symbolic washing machine that will cleanse your mind of what you believe has sullied it. You are coming to the conclusion of the dream, being vigilant for all the remaining stains that need to be washed clean. It is doable, just as mt dreamed. When you woke up, you were pleased the dream machine was "cleaning its last load."

Enjoy your day at the gallery. It will unfold with My guidance, step by step, moment by moment. It is already accomplished. Smile at mt. She is held in love, as is every being in the universe.

51

What Do You See?

*There are only two ways of viewing the world—
through the eyes of perception, or through My Vision.*

February 22, 2014

Holy Spirit, what is Your instruction? You are one with Me and we
are together in the flow. You see the life of the dream passing
before your eyes, yet you feel Me within as unmoving. I am the
only Constant in your life. Everything else changes by the second.
The calm ocean you swam in yesterday morning was bursting
with huge swells last night. Nothing remains the same in the
world, but I am always there. God never changes. God is forever.
You no longer need to hear Me speak, or whisper in your ear, to
know I am with you. We are together from morning to night and
while you sleep. I supply all your needs, and you trust that My
perfect plan is being revealed. Nothing in your life is out of place.
We exist as one, although the recognition of Me as your Self
cannot yet be fully experienced. That will come in its own time.
For now, just enjoy each moment of each day.

You wonder what we are to write next as a buzzing fly lands
on your computer screen. It is annoying to mt because she wants
"perfect peace" for the scribing. This is the condition of your
world, which you read about in the *Course* last night. Essentially,
the passage declared that everything, every image, every thought
in the dream of separation, is an act of murder. This is difficult to
accept at first, yet it is clear you would "murder" the fly to get it
off your screen. Everything on the movie screen of the mind is an
image of death, a symbol of separation when seen through the
eyes of the ego. You have also been told that everything is a

thought of love. There are only two ways of viewing the world—through the eyes of perception, or through My Vision.

You realize in this moment that the "annoying" fly was really an object of My Love to help you understand the passage you read in the *Course*. And yes, you have never in all your years had a fly buzzing on your computer screen. Only by rising above the distressing world are you able to witness a fly with the eyes of love. You smile at its presence and thank it for the gift of My message. Yes, everything in the imagined world can be seen as a messenger bringing symbols of My Presence to you. Even a lowly fly will welcome your love and will leave your screen after you acknowledge it. And for the readers, the fly has left, nowhere to be seen or heard. This is the purpose of living with Me above the battlefield and watching the dream unfold.

Everything in its duality can be seen as hate or love—interchangeable opposites from moment to moment. Special love in a relationship becomes special hate. There is only one way to recognize the true love that exists beyond all form, and that is through My Vision from above where you make the choice to see your brother as your Self. The brother is a direct reflection of all that is in your mind. Because there can be no separation in God, no relationship "with another" in this world of form can be real. You believe your brother is different from you, better or worse, richer or poorer, more or less talented. The goal is to look with My interpretation and see he is just a mirror image of the thoughts you carry about your self. Unexpressed and unacknowledged thoughts are always projected onto the brother. He is your computer screen, which can be either a place of acceptance, when recognized as an expression of Me to wake you up, or rejection, like the bug on your screen you see as a scourge of the devil. And, if that is how you see it, release it as just an image trying to divert and distract you from your only purpose—to wake up.

The world of form is a means to keep you from your truth. Mt was hopping up and down, turning on lights to shoo the fly off the screen when our writing began. She was able to return to her computer to find Me still there, and the sentence ready to be completed. I am Constant throughout all the distractions of your ego mind. Nothing can keep Me from you. With every disturbing thought, come to Me, and ask to rise above the screen of your mind. Watch those thoughts and images while being held in My total Love and acceptance. Your perception will be changed, and you can welcome the other with love, merely a part of your mind that needed to be recognized. Then it vanishes, as did the little fly messenger, which has not returned. Peace reigns.

52

Burn, Baby, Burn

*All parts of your life are symbolic of the fire of Love
that now consumes you.*

February 23, 2014

Holy Spirit, what is Your instruction this morning? You have come to a deeper understanding of your ego thought system. You awakened this morning with a dream of being in a room of smokers. You were surprised that a public gathering place allowed smoking and even counted the number of people who smoked. You were not outraged or upset by it; you just observed, though not aware of any smell. You wondered why this was happening. When you woke up, I told you the smokers were the out pictures of "that in you which is burning." Where there is smoke, there is fire. You are now reminded of the painting of the mongoose in the burning cane field that always brought you to tears.

For more than twenty years, you have been burning up with frequent hot flashes. As you wrote down My interpretation, you experienced a severe hot flash and felt it was a sign that what I said was true. Yes, the smokers represent the burning up of your ego thought system, and now you truly see it for what it is. Your Sufi teacher had asked you to be his "Daughter of Fire" and write a book about him, as Irina Tweedy had written about her Sufi master. You had loved reading how she reached enlightenment in the heat of India through her own internal burning. You wanted to be that one and were willing to go through the torture of heat to reach the goal. When I asked you to move to Maui, eleven years ago, at first you responded, "I don't want to live on a hot little island, since I am overcome with hot flashes already," but you gave your assent.

You do see how the ego is burning up, symbolized in your present loss of resistance to the continuous hot flashes. You have surrendered to My assistance in the burning of a thought system that has held you in the confines of symbolic hell on earth, for lifetimes. The ego has to be willingly released, and you have allowed the burning to take place without intervention or protest. You have not medicated or cursed the hot flashes after enduring them as just part of life these many years. You accepted they were part of your transformative process, and you could let them occur without a fuss. Every image you see is to be placed in that inner furnace for the burning; every image is ready for the conflagration. You think of Rumi's symbol of the moths being drawn to the flame, which incinerates them. This is an image of you in My furnace. No wonder you are living on the slope of a dormant volcano. The burning is under your feet, as well as in your belly and your heart. All parts of your life are symbolic of the fire of Love that now consumes you.

You had never thought in terms of "a fire of love," but that is what surrounds you. *Like a past life of being burned at the stake?* Yes, but now you are dying before you die. All the images of all lifetimes are set aflame. None has any value. Nothing matters but the burning, burning everything till the last ember dies. I tend the fire and know how to regulate the furnace that contains the fuel. I turn the temperature up and down as necessary to make sure you are perfectly cooked for your transfer into a new estate. Everything is ready, and the timer is set for you to leave this earth with absolutely no attachments, nothing left to hold you. You do not need to have endless years of hot flashes or live in a stifling hot environment to reach Nirvana. You only need to release all that would hold you to the body and mind of the ego thought system.

This is a big order. It means you must be willing to let go of everything you still believe is real, everything except your Oneness with Me. I am the representative of God in you, your Christ Self. Only this is real within the experience of your life in form. When that is fully "burned up," you are left with nothing but your true Self. There are no more movies of lifetimes on earth—past, present, or future. Time no longer exists. This is beyond the ego's capacity to imagine. The Divine Fire has brought you Home. You are, in this moment, safely held in the arms of the Father, Whom you never left. The books are just one of the maps to take you there. They are a gift to humanity and are serving the mind, and Me, well. I thank the three of you for your attentive, loving work. Now we go further.

53

I Am My Brother

Learn the greatest lesson of this life:
your brother is you; you are the same.

February 24, 2014

Holy Spirit, what is Your instruction today? We will write about the meeting you had yesterday with your close friend Marie, who took a hiatus from our work when the thought of this world being a dream became too threatening to her ego. She would still attach to her life, which gives her great satisfaction as the caretaker of her grandchild and niece. All her family interactions call her to service, filling up her time and her inner mind-space. She now has had experiences that have undeniably demonstrated to her that only by seeing the world of form, which is fraught with fear and danger, as just a dream, is she free of any harm. When Marie took her hiatus, you were not sure whether she still would continue as executor of your estate, a role that was vitally important for you to have "covered" by someone in whom you had ultimate trust. Before choosing an executor, you had hoped that person would also love the books and handle all that was required to get them to the proper source after your death. You realized when Marie told you months ago that she was "through with your project" that you had deeply depended on her as a resource of support in your life. This tie had to be cut.

Since you last interacted with Marie about the books, she has come far in her realization that this is, indeed, a world of dreams. She was given two experiences that allowed her to see the world more clearly. Several weeks ago, as she drove to the airport to pick up her sister, she was broadsided on the highway, which left her in a position for a fatal accident. I gently moved her car out of the way. During this maneuver, Marie was with Me "outside the dream" and watched the whole event from above. She saw it was clearly an illusion, and knew she was safe in My hands. On your way to meet her on the beach yesterday morning, you saw the driver's side of her car that was deeply dented and scraped from hood to tailpipe.

Marie also shared a dream where she was fully aware of the falsity of this ego world, but when she tried desperately to communicate that understanding to her many siblings, no one would listen. You made My interpretation clear that she is being given unmistakable lessons to acknowledge she is, in fact, the dreamer of her dream. Her only salvation is to rise above it with Me and watch the ego dramas unfold in the world below. Marie's need for a break was to give her the opportunity to see that she is deeply connected with Me, independent of you, the books, or any element she would "worship" in the world. She has her own way of being with Me and needs to rely on that experience, regardless of what anyone tells her. I will direct her in My Way.

After your meeting, I said you were to see Marie as a reflection of yourself, but not to be dependent on her to serve you, according to your earthly needs. Yes, I have chosen her to be the executor of your estate, which serves Me, but her role is not to be a caretaker for you in your dying days. That, I have handled, and you still have many years ahead of you. There is to be no concern about anything in this world—everything is covered, right down to the minutest detail. Your time of death is set. It will happen easily and without pain. Marie will fulfill her role as executor, and you need not worry; you will already have left this earth plane. Yes, smile at it all now with Me.

It was also necessary for you to step back from Marie. Your ego made it appear as just the opposite, that Marie was retreating from you. Marie is your projection, just as you are hers, mirrors of each other, selves that were to reunite in this time and place to fulfill a role. It is not about the mundane tasks of caring for family or managing the mechanics of dealing with property after death. It is about both of you awakening simultaneously to the awareness that I am your true Self. In the dream, it appears you are separate beings, sometimes at odds, but that is a trick of the ego. It will always intercede to protect its life. When you see Marie as one and the same as you, the ego has lost. It survives on separation and judgment. You allowed Marie to take leave with the understanding she was part of you, and you were both doing My Will. Her return and desire to once again hear some of the book's passages is an opportunity to learn the greatest lesson of this life: your brother is you, and you are the same. Beyond form, you are the One Son, and nothing separates one part of the Son from another.

On the earth plane, it may appear you are fulfilling different roles in different places, but in My Heart, we are joined for eternity. I have chosen you both to be here on Maui, with Me as your focus, to fulfill My mission for you. How this looks to the eyes of perception makes no difference. You are My messengers bringing Love to each other and to your world. This may not be apparent in form, but it is taking place in the mind. Go about your lives as you have been doing, asking, and listening for My guidance. We are all One with God.

54

Hologram of Humanity

*Nothing you perceive is real—just images that
appear to make sense.*

February 25, 2014

Holy Spirit, what is Your instruction today? You have been looking
more carefully at the dream world. Yesterday, you read excerpts
from a new book, which described the journey to knowing Me,
but for you, it was laden with far too much complication, too
much focus on the earth world. You prefer "your" path to Me
because it feels more direct. Together, we witness the world as
unreal, and then you release it to Me. The world will always need
to be dealt with on any journey to awakening, and it will be
"handled" in as many ways as there are people on the planet. To
you, our way seems clear and simple, yet you must remember, it
has taken you a lifetime in form, plus thousands upon thousands
of lifetimes before this one, to reach the place of hearing My Voice
and knowing Me as your Self. You clearly see there is nothing to
judge in all the other approaches—each is the perfect way for the
dreamer and his many selves to awaken. You, Jo, and Meera are
describing a route that is working for you and will work for
millions of others. You have shown that three ordinary women,
without any mystical experiences, could support each other to
find all the layers of ego that have blocked My Voice and My
Presence and release them with My help. This is the way I have
given you to reach the point of awakening and return Home.

Yes, we can laugh at the dream and all its silly permutations.
You are getting more agile and more able to rise above the
battleground with Me and watch the ego shenanigans. When the

One Son split into "billions of cells," every aspect displayed the ego characteristics, from the basest to the most sublime that make up every human being. They all exist in you and in your brother because you each have within you every part of the hologram of humanity, all its many faces. In reality, there is only one Face, One Christ, One Son. The rest is merely a projection of the billions of iterations of ego consciousness. Nothing you perceive is real—just images that appear to make sense.

Now is the time to see the whole movie for what it is, a depiction of life with only one goal: to awaken from it and return Home to the memory of God. Remember, only One Son "left Home." Only One Son was cast forth in the Big Bang event of the mind, which seemed to produce a universe of beings, separate and independent. And now is the time for the return, the implosion of billions of imaginary cells that all will collapse, not unlike the outcropping of annoying black gnats in your living room that will die tomorrow when their life cycle ends.

55

Beyond Earthly Treasures

Money becomes the idol of the people
and a major substitute for God.

February 26, 2014

Holy Spirit, what is Your instruction? You have had a night of extremely valuable realizations. You see that a primary projection of yours—the bank—is also one of the world's prime projections of fear. Yesterday, you spent time with your financial planner, a man filled with light and joy who has given you a sense of liberation regarding your future. He assured you that not only do you have enough finances to live out the rest of your life, you can also afford to be generous to yourself. Yesterday, he reminded you how "tight" you appeared when you first met, holding on to all you had, fearing there would not be enough. Now you display openness and happiness, the complete opposite. He was actually describing the whole spiritual journey here.

You all come in, tightly knit to the ego thought system of fear and scarcity and enter a world that would take what you have. You fear God will take away your individuality and your life in form, so you hold it close to your heart as all you will ever have. In this belief, your life becomes symbolized by the money, or lack thereof, in your possession. You become obsessed with having more of everything so your life can be easily sustained. Money becomes the idol of the people and a major substitute for God. You image now all the Olympians biting their gold medals; money is the "real" spiritual food of the planet.

With this in mind, it only makes sense that "the bank," the holder of all the money, would be the ultimate symbol for heaven.

Yes, "heaven" is entered through the golden gates, and its streets are paved with gold. Drop the *L* of gold and you have *God*. The home to which you long to return is a place of treasures and riches beyond your imagination—the Biblical imagery of God's Kingdom. And yes, "kingdom" denotes a place of kings and golden crowns. Last night, you saw a clip of the news where the Bank of the Vatican is sovereign, a holder of the riches of many kingdoms, states, and countries, yet it is corrupt. Everything in the world of form has its opposite. For you, the bank has symbolized both fear and solace. Your father was the treasurer of a small bank and keeper of the vault. In the art society, you hold the keys to the old courthouse and know the combination for the safe— symbolically the keys to the treasure house of God, the keys to His Heavenly Kingdom.

Over the years, your bank in Maui has lost the aura of fear and tension for you. Every time you walk in, you are greeted lovingly, delighted that all the tellers and staff recognize you. They do like you, and you feel the same toward them. Your financial planner has shown you that you will live comfortably to the end of your days. You feel competent to enter the vault and open your safe deposit box because the bank has become a place of safety, protection, and comfort for you. Now that the peace of God is within your heart, the fear associated with the bank is gone. As you have evolved in your relationship with Me, you have also seen an evolution in your relationship with the bank. It is no longer a devouring monster, as seen by a world in financial crisis; for you, it represents a place of love and plenty. The bank, as everything else in the dream, is purely symbolic. You are the banker, just as you are the dreamer of the dream. I am the Bank, the Banker, and treasure of your soul, the golden heart of who you are. When you see Me as your Self, you see everything as a reflection of the Self, constant and loving, offering you abundance at every turn.

This early morning, you had a dream of pulling out the file drawer in your desk. There were no files, just some winter clothes, mittens, a woolen hat, and a beautiful woven dress. You wanted to offer them all to Claudia, but she could not use it. She was your Denver friend and a former patient on the dialysis unit who chose to leave this world rather than return to treatment when her kidney transplant failed. She was as committed to the spiritual journey as were you, and both of you were followers of Sai Baba at the time. You watched her closely, over the final days of her life, as she let go of every attachment, carefully distributing her earthly treasures to those she loved. The light of her being became brighter and stronger each day, and you could not keep yourself from its embrace. You were present at her moment of death, which was peaceful and holy. When her family later held a memorial gathering at their home, you met Meera, Claudia's next door neighbor. Claudia did complete the work of this life and handed you the torch through an experience you and Meera had a few years later in your home when you independently saw Claudia's eyes appear in each other's eyes. That experience began your "joint journey" on a path that led to an in-depth study of the *Course*, the hearing of My Voice, and, soon after, the commencement of our books.

You are all placed exactly where you are supposed to be. Each one you encounter is here for a specific purpose. The purpose is Mine, which I unfold. Claudia was to return Home in the moment she did, and you were to meet Meera to complete your work with Me, in this lifetime. You no longer need the files or the clothes of this life. Nothing here has value. The bank is merely another symbol that will vanish. You know it is not the holder of what you value most in the world. All that matters now is your relationship with Me. You witnessed Claudia at the end of her life, focused only on her love of God. She is the mirror for you, Meera, and Jo. Each of you is on the way to completing this dream journey with Me, your Guide and your truth.

(After receiving this message, I thought of the Bible passage from Matthew 6: "Do not store up for yourselves treasures on earth, where moths and vermin destroy, and where thieves break in and steal. But store up for yourselves treasures in heaven, where moths and vermin do not destroy and where thieves do not break in and steal. For where your treasure is, there your heart will be also.")

56

Happy Dreaming

The happy dream is an out picture of the joy you experience when you feel Me in your heart.

February 28, 2014

Holy Spirit, my Self, what is Your instruction? We will begin with your dream of the morning where strangers from other countries wanted you to be their teacher. You had no hesitation or agenda and were willing to do whatever was asked. In fact, you were glad you would be available. In the dream, you witnessed the request and your unquestioned willingness, which is the state of your life now. This is how it will continue. I place you where I will, and you are happy to perform whatever task I set before you. That is what you do each day with the writing. You have no question it is your assignment and no idea how the message will unfold.

You are My ready vehicle for the work, so the people and places you encounter are of no consequence. You welcome them and trust My agenda is being followed. That happened yesterday after you left the gallery. You were heading for your car when you met two of your selves, out pictures of the state you now inhabit. The first was a handyman driving his truck near the tree where you had just picked a beautiful red cherry. There was no apparent reason for him to slow down and speak to you on the little road, but he did. It was then you noticed a poster of the Ten Commandments covering the driver-side door. He spoke to you about his relationship with the Holy Spirit, how I had healed his life, and how he was filled with gratitude. You gave him the cherry and told him to plant the seed in his new retirement garden. He was Me, coming to greet you in an expression of humility and adoration, a mirror of who you represent to all you see.

Next, you met a woman with a large bunch of red and yellow long-stemmed roses—clearly found in the trash but being lovingly carried in her arms as she rode her bike. You spoke to her of the roses and learned of your connection having both been wedding florists. Then her face lit up, and she joyfully exclaimed, "I love myself!" and held up the ring she had bought to commemorate that feeling. The woman on the bike was also Me embracing you with the joy of our wedding. You ask if I really mean to say this because it is what "you" would say. Yes. We are one and the same, and one with every character who appears in your day or nighttime dreams. You are clearer than ever that your life is only a dream. This time, though, it felt different, a dream of joy. You loved the characters in your night dream, as well as the man in the truck, and the woman on the bike. Everyone and everything— including the bright, juicy cherry and the fading bouquet of roses—is a reflection of you.

Yesterday morning, you had the experience of wanting to incorporate all the beauty and joy you see. You compared it with the statement that mothers and families often use for a sweet new baby when they say, "I love you so much I could eat you up." This is the feeling "to be with Me as your all and everything" engenders. After yesterday's message, you realized the objects of your desire were nothing other than the expression of your lifetimes of longing to return to Me, Home, to God. Now that you know Me as a constant Source of Love within, you would "consume" every image and thought of the dream. You take it all in: the beauty of the mountains, the banyan tree, all the people in the gallery, on the street and sidewalks, the fruit of the trees, and, yes, that little turtle you replaced in the koi pond after picking it up, looking into its green eye, and telling it how much you love it. This is the new world of the happy dream, which is still a dream, and you know it as that. It is purely a mirage, an out picture of the joy you experience because you now feel the incorporation of Me in your heart as your Self.

57

A Gathering of Selves

Look on all things with a gentle smile.

March 1, 2014

Holy Spirit, what is Your instruction? You just had a dream where friends and acquaintances were all sitting at a round wooden table. Each person was dressed for a party, bright and shiny, clearly happy to be there. You were not seated and were an observer without form. The table members began to increase in number, and a couple you had recognized seemed to merge into the new arrivals. You also noticed some of your mother's friends, familiar faces whose names were long forgotten. Others were totally unfamiliar. Soon the table was filled, but you just stayed present and watched. There was no real interaction to speak of among those gathered. When you woke, you immediately thought of the return of the many selves. Yes, that is correct. It was just a happy event, a random gathering of the players in your life. There was nothing that made one more valuable than another.

This is the state of your life now—the selves are fast returning. They are coming together to acknowledge the final scene of the movie, without the hullabaloo of the Oscar awards, and each has played their part well. Not one is special, no one better or worse than another. You wonder about the dozens of people who have played major roles in your life but who were not represented at the table. It doesn't matter who shows up. Each is just a manifestation of your own mind, your own thought, an out picture of your imagined self. Your ego keeps asking you why Jo, Meera, Zoe, Susan, or Tom were not there. It need not be; all are the same. This message of the day now brings tears.

All specialness is dispelled. The final gathering is nondescript. Right now, you could not name a single person in the dream except perhaps Gertie Grimes, your mother's friend who worked at an upscale grocery store and wore the purest, starched white dress you have ever seen. The ego says, "Why would she be there?" I say because her name symbolizes all the grime that has covered your shining selves, all who are part of your dream. Your slate is wiped clean now. There is nothing but Me, your Shining Self Who shows up at your "table" every day, every moment. You do get it! This was emphasized for you when you met the "God man" in the truck and the bearer of fading roses on her bicycle. They were clearly parts of you, showing up with the message that you are truly in a new place.

Yesterday, after you had already talked with your friend Andy twice, he called again with a question from Me. I had told him to ask you about "the bank." Andy said he had been thinking that "a bank is an idol." You immediately put aside your taxes to share with him the writing of three days ago about the bank as an idol and the Bank as Self. This was a sign to him that I am in charge of the writing, and I disseminate it for the benefit of mankind. Then you heard from your friend Nikki, who emailed that she is trying to understand the two messages you sent her earlier in the week. Yes, the messages are challenging to the ego, especially when the reader has no background in the *Course*, but I work with each one to help him achieve full understanding.

Everyone you see is just a projection, seeking the light of knowledge. You are bringing the light to each self within the mind in your love of Me. The love we share is being extended to every aspect of the mind, but not until now are you truly making that connection. You experience the peace and joy of this message and are taking it in at a whole new level. It is the "truth" of the dream state you currently inhabit. You will now witness with Me all aspects of your dream life from the role of observer. Each character, whether human or otherwise, reflects what is in your mind. Even the little crabs that pop up from the crevices of the rocks to greet you are reminding you that I am in everything you lay your eyes on; everything is a manifestation of the Thought of God, all made of Love.

Look on all things with a gentle smile and know they offer you their gratefulness for the return now taking place. This is the meaning of the gathering at the table—everyone is returning home in your mind. They show up in recognition and gratitude that the end of the dream is near. You feel the relief of knowing that everything is settled, and there is nothing to cause concern or harm. The players are on their way home. In the end, they will merge into the One Son. The awakening of the mind will allow you to see that the world was never real, but it served its purpose to open all eyes to the truth of their oneness beyond form.

58

Collapse of the Ego Thought System

You are with Me, and the ego feels forsaken.

March 2, 2014

Holy Spirit, what is Your instruction? We will write of the dream you had this morning. In it, you were alone, an observer in a place you had never encountered. You were standing on top of a steep and grassy hill looking down on what appeared to be a metal "stadium" set deep into the ground. No seats covered the skeletal foundation, yet it seemed like it could hold an audience. At the base of the structure, huge crabs, some flesh-colored, were hungrily ascending the sides, eager to get a better view. You looked over your right shoulder and saw nothing but water, hundreds of feet below. Although you intensely felt the fear of falling over the edge, you also had the desire to "get it over with"—something inside of you wanted to cast yourself into the "nothingness." You believed you could not survive in this place, living so close to "the end of the world" as it appeared to you. You felt no attachment to the huge crabs, about eight of them, that had escaped the confines of the dark cavern beneath the structure. The only sign of human life was a friend planting sticks on the side of the hill, but there was no real connection with her. You were truly alone with a useless structure before your eyes, the call of death to your right, and nothing to hold you to this place.

As we reviewed the dream together, you understood that you were viewing the death of the whole ego thought system. There was nothing left of it to attract you. Nothing to engage you. The only impetus was your desire to fall from the heights into the void to your death in the water below. You are with Me now, and the ego feels forsaken. It has lost its structure, and its mt character no longer wants its world. I am the only holder of mt's life. She is purely a vehicle to serve My purpose, to view the fearful world now with the thought of love. Your dream depicts the shift you have made from the ego thought system to Me, as your Teacher, Friend, Lover, and Self. Nothing else exists. The fleeing crabs represent a world seeking liberation, hungry to go beyond its cave-like existence in the dark.

Yes, you are reminded of Plato's Cave. Without fear, humanity would leave the cave and be free. You represent a beacon of freedom to the crabs coming out of their cavern to take them beyond the structures of form and into the light of liberation. The sensation of "fear" you felt, as you first woke, is again filling your chest, but now it's seen as the experience you often have, in your sternum, when you feel My Presence. Yes, I took away the thought of fear, a sign the ego thought system has all but collapsed. You will continue to "need it" the rest of your earthly life, but its structures are now barren of anything you would want to cling to. Nothing here attracts or serves you. You are in My Power, operating from My Presence and Love. Take this in.

59

A Threatened Ego

A strong bond with Me assures you that
nothing can go wrong.

March 3, 2014

Holy Spirit, what is Your instruction this morning? The desire of your ego for you to stay small and limited is the present challenge of your life in the dream. The ego cannot deal with the expansion taking place in your consciousness and would reject all learnings of Me and from Me. There is still a battle being waged internally as your ego fights for its life. We are working to collapse the perceived universe of form, and you have a strong bond with Me. This assures you that nothing can go wrong. Today, you will be sending some of our messages to Carol Howe, who will be a vehicle for their extension into the world. This is most threatening to your ego.

Last night you had a significant dream that clearly portrayed your role as teacher, a position you have played throughout lifetimes. But in the dream, you were in a more powerful role than usual: a Teacher of God, as described in *A Course in Miracles.* You were at a college, talking with one of its most beloved instructors and felt paired with her in some way. Although you were not a professor, you held a special role in the school where you worked, demonstrating and teaching the principles of the *Course,* which you deeply loved. You understood that enlightenment can be had by all. It was a delight to be together so impersonally with another teacher, someone who was also seeking the way home. You knew your joy would not come from just teaching the *Course* but by living it.

Your sister Susan, in her prophetic voice, once said to you about My words, "You will be teaching this." She felt it would not be limited to just those few who are now receiving samples of the messages. Yes, the expansion is at hand, and the role of "teacher" for you, Jo, and Meera is set in motion. You have been "demonstrating" the results of all the work you have done to take back projections. Whether this can be acknowledged by those who see the changes in you, makes no difference. You each know the peace that enters your lives daily.

Carol Howe will read the three messages you are sending her today and give you encouragement in putting them out into the world. Even though your ego would like to stop the process, it can't because this is your next step in trusting that I have everything handled. Do not make up any stories about who will help you or how the help will come. Your limited ego mind does not make this happen. I am in charge. You each have your own unique role and it will become clear. Right now, you are completing the necessary tasks that will set you free to focus fully on Me. Send Carol the pages we have selected and wait for her response. You will be guided to the next step. Yes, your anticipation is great. I have cleared the mind of mental distractions, fears, and assumptions so that you can hear My Voice and follow My Will. Open to the bounty that awaits you every second you walk with Me.

60

Meet Your Self Everywhere

You are not real; you live in a realm of dreams.

March 4, 2014

Holy Spirit, what is Your instruction? You had another significant dream last night to show you how far you have come. You dreamed that you and your youthful mother were in a huge mountain basin. She was above you on one of the ridges, and you were somewhere below. You had no real sense of your body, or even of touching the ground, but you were aware of seeing your beautiful mother enjoying her walk. You were also noticing the wispy clouds flying near the tops of the 14,000 foot mountains surrounding you. There was no sense of having any destination. All of a sudden, you found yourself deep in the middle of a huge city with towering buildings that blocked out the sun and sky. One building was a Sears, but other than that, nothing was familiar. You had no idea how you could ever find your mother or how she could ever find you, but you stayed calm, stood on the curb, and prayed. As you lifted your head, your mother, in all her beauty and poise, stood in front of you. There had been no panic, and it felt absolutely natural that she should appear in that moment. You knew your prayer had been answered. And that is now the way of everything.

Not until after I had interpreted the dream did you realize it was to be the final resolution of your mother's recurring dream of being lost in a big city that she often repeated at the breakfast table during your childhood. You realize that her dream represented the original separation. The pain you felt for her, at each telling, was really your own pain of being separated from

God, lost in a world of form from which there is no way out. You do know your mother is your projection. Her profound sense of abandonment from all she loved in this life was really your sense of leaving Heaven. When you reunited with your mother in the big city, the two of you became one. She was not lost; she found her way directly to you, and you trusted that I was the One Who had interceded. Your mother appeared calm and showed no surprise at meeting you exactly where she did. Yes, she is a figment of the imagined separation, but she returned "home" to join with you, her holy Self. You know I orchestrate the return of all the many selves. A major experience of the return is to rejoin with one's mother—the imagined vehicle of the separation through birth.

You smile as you think of the book *Friday,* written by Robert Heinlein. It is about a genetically engineered AP, an "Artificial Person," whose name just happens to be yours: Marjorie. She has been implanted with a fetus, which she is to deliver to the Ruler of the Realm. You love reading about the false self at the same time you are getting more clarity that you, in fact, are not real and live in a realm of dreams. Even though there were only a few pages left to the book, you were falling asleep, so you had to end the reading on page 333. You were amazed to notice the page number. That same number had arisen time and time again throughout your day. When you and Jo were deciding which messages to send to Carol Howe, Jo mentioned that it was 3:33 p.m. in Denver. You told her that the date was 3/3. Much later, after a meeting at the bank, you found yourself directly behind a car with the license plate 333.

Yesterday, you emailed Carol three examples of our daily dictation. The first one was specifically dedicated to the joining of you, Jo, and Meera. Yes, you are My triad, and without the three of you, the books would never have been written. It has taken three, just as Helen had to be in communication with Bill and Ken to put *A Course in Miracles* into the world. You needed each other to ground and assimilate the transmissions coming from Me to you. This was essential for producing the books and for your joint awakening from the dream. Be happy the three of you were able to send the writing to Carol, who loves Me and who is also sharing My *Course* with the world through her teaching.

It is a joy to be joined and, especially, to share the results of the joining. I emphasized 333 yesterday as a number, a page, the time of day on a clock. Form does not matter. Marjorie, the AP, described in a book, is no different from "mt" who reads the book. The mother in your dream is also you, one and the same. You met with love under My auspices and direction. See everyone you meet as a mirror of your holy Self—the One Son of God. The fleeting clouds have exposed the beauty of the mountain heights, which now can be easily reached.

61

One Face

Look at everyone with My Vision
and you will see a new world.

March 5, 2014

Holy Spirit, what is Your instruction today? You are feeling a sense of the real world, a different "life" than you have known to this point. In it, all the characters are coming to joy, peace, and completion because you are coming to your completion of the journey of lifetimes. You found that it was only a dream. The journey without distance is ending, right where it began. Yesterday, you met your mother in a symbolic night dream of being lost and abandoned. This time, she knew the way to find you and reunite with you—the love of her life. It was symbolic of your meeting with Me, the Love of your life, the Breath of your being, the Treasure of your heart. I am your One and Only. You now cast off all the costumes you have ever worn: daughter, mother, sister, brother, father, great-grandfather Lewis, all your friends and acquaintances known and unknown to you. You are every single one of them. Replace the face of your mother, in yesterday's dream, with their faces, and know they represent the only face there is—the face of Christ, which each and every one represents. The dream of you and your mother in the big city is about the reunion taking place in the mind with everyone. It is happening with joy, yet a mere reflection of the Joy that will be felt when you experience the return to Heaven. Yes, this is heaven on earth.

Look at everyone with My Vision and you will see a new world, a happy world where the people you love come to peace and wholeness, regardless of their life circumstances. Your friend Zoe has let you know there is not an opening for "face to face" contact. You understood her need to be separate in form, and you both reiterated you are forever together in the heart. The Heart is the Mind of God, and the connection with every being rests there. You are able to fully acknowledge the state of peace and acceptance, the feeling of being at Home, One with what is. Nothing can throw you off track. Yesterday, Meera sent you and Jo the song lyrics she will use in her next Nia class: "Just hold on, we're going home." She felt such joy that its message will be transformative to all who hear it. This, too, is the reflection for the three of you that the happy dream is now the core of your life, the internal embrace of Me. The abundance of God is what you are sensing, but it is a mere shadow of what you will know when you have left the world and return Home. You have awakened in the dream and will fully awaken from it. As yet, this concept is beyond your full comprehension, but you are getting there.

Today, turn every errant thought over to Me. There is absolutely no cause for concern about anything your ego self could possibly imagine. You are still living in a dream, but your Self recognizes it as nothing other than a mirage. The ego "still exists" in this imaginary world while your body requires sustenance and shelter. Smile at it, and witness it from above, with Me. You know I am your only true Self. As we watch the movie of this life, you "get the picture" that there is really nothing of substance in the universe. It is all made up and will soon collapse. All readers are receiving the transmission of these words. It will give them the help they need to find Me so I can assist them in their awakening process. You will all awaken, and you will all return Home, just as I have promised, even in the lyrics of a song: *Just hold on. We're going home; it's hard to do these things alone. Just hold on. We're going home.*

62

Fear of No Return

*The belief that God will not accept you
is the last fear to be released.*

March 6, 2014

Holy Spirit, what is Your instruction today? You have come to the real world, but you don't know it as such. That's all right. It will take getting used to. You have found yourself in a "new world," one that allows you to access Me at any moment and to see your brother as your Self. This was the goal you set out to achieve and what you now witness. You desired to come home to Me and you have. You smile because you just finished reading the book *Friday* where "Marjorie, the Artificial Person" migrates to another planet and serendipitously finds her lost, best, and only friends as part of the migrant cargo on her spaceship. The last words in the book are "Yes, I belong. It's a warm and happy feeling." This is the way life works—everything on your mind screen reflects where you are on the path. It was no accident you finished the book last night because yesterday you had a deep recognition of how far you, Jo, and Meera have come on the journey to Me. Another major confirmation was ushered in by Carol Howe, who emailed you that she had received the document you sent of our daily messages. When she said she will "delve deeply into them," you were overwhelmed with tears of relief and gratitude.

Why did Carol's letter touch me so deeply? Your deep-seated fear of rejection was met with love. In your mind, Carol represents salvation, a home for the books, a womb of acceptance and love. The books are your extension into the world of the deepest love you know, and yes, you want to see them embraced by her the way we hold them so dear. You feel her warmth and receptivity, which is My Love reflected in her. She is the reflection of you, and she will receive the messages. Your fear arose with the belief that God will not really accept you, that He will still find some flaw and will not take you back. This is the last fear to be released. To you, Carol is the one who most closely represents Me since you both know Me through the *Course.* I accept you; Carol, as your Self, accepts you. God welcomes your return. You never left Him.

This message has already had a profound effect on your consciousness. It has allowed you to rise above the battlefield to see your soul's longing to return to love and see your deepest fear that you could never return. This is the condition of every man. You "groked" it, as Heinlein would say, meaning you fully and completely understood with every fiber of your being, that the fear that binds you to planet Earth is the fear your love will not be accepted. Yes, this is it. The little book about "Marjorie, the AP," migrating from earth to a place that would embrace her in the love of family, has essentially the same message. You have to face your deepest fear that you will be rejected by God and then see that belief through My Vision to know it carries no truth. The truth is, you have always been held in God's Love, and you are purely that. You receive My Love in the daily dictation, and Carol, as your mirror, received My messages and welcomed them with love. This you must trust. Even with My Presence so firmly established within you, the ego will fight every proclamation of love, whatever its source, because to it, love means its death. You looked death in the eye with the exercise of sending the writing to Carol.

Yes, it is a stretch of the mind to learn that nothing but My Love, the Love of God, exists. We are at a new level of joining and trusting. This is why I say that it is the real world, a place in the right mind of recognizing your union with Me as Love. Earlier, you were attempting to convince yourself that My assurance that Carol would welcome the writing was true, but your ego was screaming in protestation. It was well aware that your experience with her would be a turning point for a new shift of mind, a shift that would allow you to dissociate from the world of separation in the most profound way yet. You are still working to be ever vigilant for the ego's tricks, but you are so aligned with Me now that its stunts will be only blips on the screen of your mind. You can laugh at their appearance and demise. Trust Me continuously, every second, as the only interpreter of your world. I know the ways of the ego's manipulations. I am always shining My Light of Love on them, using each one as a lesson to take you another step closer to Home.

63

No Hierarchy of Illusions

You can do nothing wrong,
so you can laugh at what appears to be a mistake.

March 7, 2014

Holy Spirit, what is Your instruction? We will look at the experience you had yesterday when you went to the annual meeting of your condo owners to vote. Nothing out of the ordinary seemed to be happening, yet it was important for you to be present. For some reason, you did not read the ballot instructions. You just voted for yourself and an absentee condo owner. Instead of voting for three of the four candidates, as directed, you voted for all four. In the end, when the tabulation was called, an announcement was made that three people had invalidated their ballots by voting for all the candidates. Everyone laughed—but you. Actually, you did not feel shame or guilt, remembering *there is no hierarchy of illusions.* Yes, this was the real message of the meeting. All the candidates were equal. Not one could have been selected over another in the state of mind you now inhabit. You did exactly what would be called for in the real world where all beings are the same, each a mirror of the One Christ Self.

This is the way of your new life. You do march to a different drummer, and I am that One. We look on everything in the world as equal, created of Love. Whether you voted or not made no difference; all votes are invalidated in the real world. There is nothing to vote for when all are the same. You had to have that lesson yesterday, even though it may seem improbable to you that it wasn't just a mistake of your inattentive mind. I am the One operating every minute aspect of your life, and because you do

229

know that, you were able to let go of the whole voting scenario. There is nothing you can do wrong, so you get to laugh at what appears to be a mistake. Join the whole audience in laughter. Better yet, join above it all and laugh with Me.

You have lived in this world of form in its many iterations over the centuries, but now you see it with new eyes, through My Vision. The edges are not as sharp in this softened world, and nothing here should be taken seriously. You can smile at all the arguments over how to spend the budget, regardless of whose budget is being described—the world governments, your condo complex, or your personal estate. Who cares? Only the ego, and it would make every aspect of your life into something serious and potentially threatening. Nobody lost and no one gained from your canceled ballot. It does not matter who you favor or who favors you or us. What matters is that I am Known as the One Who is the Truth of your Being, the One Who guides you through the maze of life on planet Earth.

You feel the relief of My taking over everything in your life. You do not need to figure anything out because My Presence is there every moment holding you in Love. Any apparent mistake, which is brought to Me for immediate correction, has served a purpose beyond the scope of your limited mind. The ballot "fiasco" was a dream, a skit on the stage that will have absolutely no consequence in the end. It was a tool for Me to use for today's dictation. The point of your imagined life is to know I am all that exists, and I exist in your mind as you. We are one and the same. We are part and parcel of God, created in and of Love. I, in the form of Jesus, awakened and now am showing you, through symbols, images, and thoughts, the route to awaken to the truth of your Self as the Christ. Words can never describe the essence of what I am teaching, but as you move closer to the acceptance and reliance on Me as your Source, what I am saying will resonate with the deepest level of your soul. Embrace the truth of who you are as One with God.

64

Fullness

I speak to you through the scent of flowers, singing birds,
the sound of the waves; everything is symbolic
of our communion.

March 8, 2014

Holy Spirit, what is Your instruction this morning? One of the last big
lessons on earth is to know Me in the emptiness. I represent the
Void. That statement frightens the ego self because to it, the void
represents nothingness and death. Your greatest fear as a child
was the thought of nothingness. It made you almost sick to try to
comprehend what that really meant, even for a second. Now we
look at it through My eyes.

During the night, you woke up with a feeling of "not enough"
but that is not the same as "nothingness." You felt you could be
doing more for the books and even wondered if you were feeling
My Presence as often as you should. For a few moments, this was
very unsettling, but you went to Me for help. I let you know that
these feelings of not being, having, or doing enough were really
the out picture of the ego's trauma over its loss of your full
attention. You have given the majority of your focus to Me, and
the ego mind is feeling abandoned. It is screaming that it does not
have enough of you and wants you back. That ego fear, the loss of
"its life," is out pictured in all the situations where you, as mt,
believe you could be doing more, but that is not true.

When you returned to sleep, I gave you a dream to restore
you to your right mind. An outdoor event had been rained out
and was instead being set up in two Sunday School rooms.

Everything was being prepared with love. You entered one of the rooms and accidentally knocked over a vase containing a stalk of the most beautiful blue iris you had ever seen. It covered the length of the room. The "turnover" did not distress you, and you were easily able to replace the flower. I am the beautiful Iris of Love that fills the room of your mind. Only Love will fill the empty space, left bare after the ego's demise. This is the point of going into Stillness and entering the Void, the "containers of love"—the nothingness. You felt that love fill up the empty Sunday School rooms where the many selves would return after lifetimes of longing. Every gathering place represents the return to love of all the characters you have played or projected over eons. Love saturates everything with its embrace. When you woke from your dream, you were filled with the warmth of inclusion, the fullness of knowing "you are in the right place" and you are loved.

Today, you are going to a Japanese flower arranging class to do the most difficult arrangement, the *Rikka*—the original arrangement done by the temple priests in Japan eight hundred years ago. This will be a celebration of coming to Me as Love. The arrangement itself represents the world, but you have gone beyond the world. That was the meaning of "toppling" the vase in your dream. You topple the world of form and top it with Me— the tallest flower. Remember, everything is symbolic of our communion. I commune with you through the flowers, the singing of the birds, the sound of the waves. There is nothing that is not composed of My Love. So there is nothing to fear when you believe that death will leave you with "nothing." Death is just a transition into an experience of Love, which has no form. The ego would frighten you with the belief that you do not "exist" after you die. Yes, it is correct you will have no body; you never did. You have never left God and are immersed in His Love. You have been since the Creation.

Now you remember the dream you had in October 2011, teaching an Ikebana class full of students. Suddenly, the room was emptied, and you found yourself at a lectern with pages of notes "for the instruction of the essentials." That was the beginning of My communication with you about the coming of a book. I am the Essential, the room is empty. The only thing real is Love. Be filled with Love today. It is your Essence.

65

The Last Step

I do foreshadow what is to come.

March 9, 2014

Holy Spirit, what is Your instruction this morning? You have found the real world where your brother is your Beloved. This state of mind is out pictured in both day and night dreaming. You saw it clearly portrayed last night in a series of dreams that began with your favorite wilderness camping spot being turned into a large cabin. It reminded you of the Student Union on campus where you met Tom. In one scenario, you found yourself feeling happy, connecting with a group of disparate people. You were all gathered in the cozy cabin on top of the mountain, a place you had loved for its pristine stillness. As you spoke with those you just met, you realized there were no barriers to your interactions; any topic could be freely discussed because nothing needed to be hidden. It was an experience of joy and freedom. Then you looked out the window and saw Tom sitting under a large tree, packing up his wooden computer case. Near the case was a small wooden box in the shape of a coffin, and lying on its back was a very happy-appearing badger. You smiled at his unusual collection.

The next sequence in your stream of dreams had you climbing the barren, almost vertical slope of the mountain, wondering if you could make the last steps to the door of the cabin above you. Then Tom appeared right in front of the cabin. He extended his invisible hand, which you took, and he pulled you up. Of course, you immediately recognized the symbolism — the oft-repeated vision of the Reunion with God in Heaven. In the dream, it was Tom, your most special relationship of this lifetime,

235

who lifted you into union. The badger in him, and in you, was safely in its coffin, and you were free to love beyond all constraints of earthly duality. You both were ready to merge into oneness.

This is the last step, when you and the brother, none other than your own Self, dissolve into the Joining beyond form. That one gesture—"invisible hand to invisible hand"—symbolizes the end of the dream. Yes, I do foreshadow what is to come, and that has often been your experience of our journey together. I carry you forward, easily and gently, to the places I have prepared for you in the mind. You called for help, and the help was immediately there, ready to welcome you into union, which goes beyond anything you could possibly imagine.

Preceding your dreams last night, you underwent an exercise of forgiveness, which for you was profound because it opened the door to taking "the last step." Yesterday, at the Ikebana class, held in the nursery schoolroom of a Buddhist temple, the priest of the temple came in to observe. He walked over to where you were struggling with your arrangement, sat beside you, and told you your flower was broken. You knew that he had no knowledge of what you were doing, and your ego resented his interruption. To you, he looked very crumpled in appearance and inept in his interactions. You ignored him and he left, but your ego was still having a heyday saying that it knows better and is more advanced in every way, essentially claiming it is more enlightened than the priest. You had never met that priest before but judged him severely the moment you saw him. This is the action of mt's ego that we watch from above the battleground. Of course, you soon realized there would be a lesson forthcoming from this encounter, and you asked for immediate forgiveness.

Before going to bed, you read about the holy encounter in the *Course*, how every brother must be blessed by you because he is your Self. During the night, we reviewed your experience with the temple priest and you clearly saw that your judgment of his ineptness was just the mirror of your own believed ineptness. The priest was a perfect out picturing of your ego self. Even though he did not realize the true light of your Being, you could feel love and acceptance for him, and see his light. In this exercise, you joined beyond form, like in your dream with Tom on the mountaintop. The climb will be different for each one, and those we meet on the path will reflect the unseen parts that need to be embraced. I am using the pronoun *we* because We do make this journey together, every step of the way. I am always with you, guiding you to take the next step toward Heaven's Door. I am your True Self, and We are One for Eternity. You accept you are still at the very beginning of the journey to Know Me, although we have made significant inroads. Celebrate how far you have come, and that you will continue with Me until God lifts you up to Union with Him.

66

Testing the Holy Spirit

Your pattern of expecting rejection
by Me/God must be released.

March 10, 2014

Holy Spirit, please help me understand my relentless looking for Carol Howe's response to the dictations from Book 1, which I sent her a few days ago. You told me I was testing You. Yes, you were. That is why you have the continuous urge to check your email. Your ego would have you focus on Carol as a guru—a substitute for Me. She represents the *Course* and the one who holds the most connection to it now for you. You image her as one who is also in a place of awakening and imagine that she will relate deeply to the writing and to your journey. You have made her into a very special relationship without ever speaking to her. She is a mirror of you, in terms of your quest for Me, and your dedication to learning and teaching the concepts of the *Course*. She is also a mirror of your Christ Self. You are now ready to look deeper at your ego's need to see the other as an object of your longing. Carol, in this instance, has become as important as God/Me in evaluating you and your worthiness. If she accepts the writing, then you are "worthy" in My eyes/God's eyes. But if she doesn't accept it, then I am no longer worthy in your eyes. You have given her the power of Knowing. She has become the one to judge the value of My messages.

You are "testing Me" by impatiently awaiting Carol's response. When I told you to send the information to her, I said she would receive it and welcome it. If she does, then I am "right." If she does not welcome it or want to connect with you or the writing, then I have "tricked and betrayed you" by telling you a lie. I can't win when Carol is in charge rather than I. You have seen this pattern all your life, waiting for the verdict of your goodness or badness, rightness or wrongness—always seeking approval and expecting rejection instead. This reflects the relationship you've had with both Tom and God in the dream of separation. No matter what you did or thought, you feared it would displease them, which would leave you in guilt. Your fear of displeasing Carol and experiencing rejection is paramount in this task of sending her the writing. Her failure to embrace it, according to the ego, will weaken your belief in Me. Then the whole world becomes real, and I, as the Power of your Being, take second place.

You can only serve one master. The ego has you serve it by projecting your connection with Me onto a special relationship in a form that "represents Me" in your mind. Carol, and her connection with the *Course*, then replaces Me. You would be allowing her to usurp My throne as the representative of your ego thought system, empowered by its need to be right, and make Me wrong. You have just been given the clearest picture yet of the ego's operation. The lesson with Carol has served you well. Stand with Me above the battlefield and laugh at how the ego would throw you off course in a situation with someone you have never even met. You must look closely at this so your pattern of expecting rejection by Me/God is once and for all released. This is also why Carol has yet not responded. You had to review this now. Remember, your longing is only for God.

Duplicity

The brother's image is a thought of betrayal.

March 11, 2014

Holy Spirit, what is Your instruction? We will look at the new territory you inhabit in the mind, now being reflected in your world. Yesterday, you had a deeper experience of knowing Me through reviewing your mistrust of Me. This is a dilemma for all humanity. Each one longs for the deepest connection to Me, but the ego thought system will do everything it can to interfere with that connection. You have been waiting for Carol Howe to respond to the daily dictations, sent over a week ago, eagerly hoping she will resonate with them, and with the three of you. You have called on Me to help you detach from your secret desire that Carol will see our endeavor as a pure reflection of the *Course*. Yes, your ego would call that recognition very special. Finally, yesterday morning, you asked Me why you cannot fully trust and just let it all unfold. You clearly heard My answer: you are testing Me. This brought you to tears. You immediately realized the truth of it, which led to a clearer understanding of your role as the mt character.

To test Me is to mistrust Me and set Me up as a betrayer of My Word, My Promise that everything is being cared for according to My Will. Your ego mind took charge of the expectations around the outcome of your sending Carol the writing. Remember, the ego lives through expectations. This is its ever-present role in your life, and you, indeed, tried to watch it and call for My help, but it got the upper hand as each day of "no response from Carol" passed. Calling on Me for the interpretation of what you had witnessed from your ego brought you to a deeper realization of its whole operation as a response to the original thought of separation.

When we looked together at what had taken place, you saw how you had bestowed on Carol the importance and power that you have assigned to Me. Her response would dictate whether My words about the way she would receive the writing were either true or false. If she embraced the messages, as I promised, then you would know you could indeed continue to trust Me. If she did not, then your ego would rejoice in believing it had toppled your faith in My enduring love, constancy, and truth. You were caught between the devil and the deep blue sea. Carol had become the substitute for God, the substitute for the Self. It would be her judgment that would make or break the trust you have developed in Me.

Every worldly action is weighed on the scale of duality. God is either a God of Love or a God of hate. There is no action you can take that will not bring the question to mind: will it cause His favor or His disfavor? You have felt that trap from early childhood, never knowing fully whether any thought or action would warrant His wrath or His forgiveness. If you became sick, you imagined you were being punished for a number of misdeeds, such as not saying your prayers or doing something that incurred guilt in a multitude of ways. You mostly believed that God watched you every moment of your life, judging you, and harshly at that. This kind of conflict was reflected in your marriage and in your friendships, where, after every sentence you spoke, you awaited the acknowledgment of its acceptability. The pattern was so routine that it became a habitual part of your consciousness, and you accepted it as "normal," if not unchangeable. Not until you have come to know My Love and Constancy have you been able to bring each and every habit to My altar for release.

You now see the whole picture of the original belief that you betrayed God, and therefore, He would find a way to betray you. This is what you have done with the example of Carol Howe. Because you value her as "one who holds the wisdom of the *Course*" and as someone connected with the original partners in its transcription, your ego mind has projected an importance onto her, which unbeknownst to you until yesterday, that was equal to My importance to you, in your mind. In that case, her "judgment" would be the projection of your judgment on your Self. This is a trick of the ego. You were not able to "see the ego at work" as it projected the thought of betrayal onto Me, through the "auspices" of Carol. Your imagined betrayal of God is what is at stake.

You did not betray God. He will never betray you. You are the Thought of God, the Love of God, and the reflection of Him in this world of form. Continue to become more aware of the predisposition of your ego thought system to project betrayal onto your brother, whose image then appears to be separate from you. Your brother is your own Self, and there is only One Son. Trust above all else that I am unfolding your life under the perfection of My direction each moment. We operate as One in the Mind and will watch the ego go through its ever-endless repetition of antics to keep you and humanity in the belief you are separate from God. That is not true. You are just having a dream, which will end as soon as this truth is fully incorporated. Embrace Me as the Voice for God and as your one and only Self. God is.

68

One Mind

What happens in "your" mind happens for all.

March 12, 2014

Holy Spirit, what is Your instruction today? You are one with Me, and that is why you are seeing the return of the many selves. Carol Howe is one of your selves, and you both were together with me in my lifetime as Jesus. It was time for the two of you to reunite with Me, which took place in the mind. After integrating her into your heart, you received Carol's acknowledgment of the transcriptions. You felt free, grateful for the realization that I am your only Master. Your desire for a connection in person with Carol was released, and you came to a deeper knowing that everything in My plan is perfect. The mind exercise of "connecting with Carol" was a vital part of the journey for you both. Whatever happens in the mind of one of you is happening in the mind you all share. This is still barely comprehensible, but you, Jo, and Meera are getting glimpses because your experiences and thoughts coincide almost daily. We are One, and this will become manifest as each day unfolds.

I am with you and every reader and every being in the dream. I am leading you each on a path that will return you to a full realization that you are One within the Mind of God. You all will remember God because My role is to awaken you to His Love. The return of the selves is underway, and the three of you are documenting that for the readers. Have no concern if those who read these pages do not comment or do not choose to associate with you again in form. Their ego self will counter these words, but their Self, which is Me, will help them to integrate their meaning beyond form. I am in the mind of every reader and resonate there as My words are read. Remember, there is a communion taking place, though it may not always be recognized. Keep doing the work of preparing these pages for dissemination and publication. Tomorrow, Meera arrives on Maui. You will join with Me in the mind and will enjoy being together in form.

69

Players on the Screen

When viewed with Me, everything you see
will be recognized as just a figment in a dream.

March 14, 2014

Holy Spirit, what is Your message? You are with Me, and strongly feel it this morning because you have joined with Meera as a reflection of your Self. You experienced "satisfaction" in the world of form, the happy dream of seeing each other in person after a long absence. It is not necessary to meet face to face to feel "joined with your brother," but it can be joyful. This you also experienced during Jo and Gary's visit, a few months ago, another reminder of your connection with Me. See everyone who appears before your eyes as the face of Christ. No one is any different from another; this is learned incrementally.

This morning, you were thinking about the President of the United States—specifically, all the wars that have ensued under his presidency and your disappointment in those decisions. I reminded you this world is not real, only a place for the lessons that are necessary to return you, and humanity, Home. You love the heart of the President, believing it is open to Me. You believe he desires what is good and right for the people, but you are concerned that peace will never manifest in a world so focused on war. That is true, but it's because the world is made only for the satisfaction of the ego. War is its food, its life. Your President will learn that reality rests only in his holy Self, beyond the world of form. You see him now as your brother, equal with you on the journey. This joining must happen for every being. They are you, and you all return Home together.

You are all homeward bound, just as is your President. The "loftiest one," along with the "least," is equal on the journey. Each will come to see that the role he plays in life, or the status he carries, has absolutely no purpose other than to provide the lessons needed to awaken him. Nothing else matters. You must awaken to the truth of your Being. I am the One Who resides within your mind. When viewed with Me, everything you think is real will be recognized as just a figment in a dream yet can be interpreted differently, as Love. Everything is composed of Love because every thought emanates from a Thought of God. This idea is getting easier for the three of you to accept, although it is not yet clear.

Jo has been upset because her cat is the one thing she thought she could depend on for comfort and affection, and now he is dying. She has called on Me repeatedly to interpret the meaning of the cancer and the meaning of death. I have assured her that Chi is beyond form and is there for her as a supreme teacher in this life. Jo will learn that death does not exist and that Chi's dying process is not causing him to suffer. Even though it has brought suffering to her, she knows it exists only in the mind. The goal of the ego is to make every man believe that death is real, and with that belief, to deny the reality of God. Jo has come to trust that My interpretation is what matters. She has released all expectations about the course her cat's "life" will take. She is able to experience him now as an "object" of pure Love. This is a reflection of Jo's love for Me. Jo, Chi, and I are one and the same. There is no loss. There is only God. This lesson is for all.

In the Mind of God, there is only Love. All that has ever existed is Love. Union takes place when this is understood. You are each experiencing your last forgiveness lessons. Mt has forgiven the President his apparent mistakes, knowing it's just how the ego perceives the world of form. The President will also awaken to the truth of his being as Love. Jo will know that Chi, a figment of her imagination, was really the out picture of My Love for her. Meera is coming to the realization that her dance is the expression of her joy in coming Home. All imagined form is collapsing into nothingness, disintegrating into Love. The time of awakening fully from the dream is approaching.

·

.

70

The Real World

I am all you desire; I fill you with My Constant Love.

March 15, 2014

Holy Spirit, what is Your instruction today? We will again speak of the real world. You still do not believe you are in such a place because you have no concept of what that means. The real world is the "space" where your only reality is Me. You imagined that the real world was outside of your mind, that it existed in the world of form, and caused the world to appear more inviting, kinder, and full of light. This idea is only the reflection of what is already taking place in your mind—*you* have become more inviting, viewing your many selves as one with you, looking on them without judgment, offering them the gifts I have given you. Therefore, you have become kinder as you shed My Light. This experience reflects the real world.

The world of form will not change; the wars will still take place, and the ego will perform its song and dance in every venue. Despite all the ways the ego encompasses the world with its passions, you remain in the stillness with Me at peace. You do experience your world differently when you look at it through new eyes, My Vision, and not your ego's perception. With My interpretation, you approach the world with love, the reflection and extension of the love you know as the Holy Spirit within. What is different is you. Now you see the forgiven world. You welcome it again and again as an opportunity to hear My Voice and do My Will. You know that every encounter and every event is planned by Me for the purpose of your return to God. You look

251

on your brothers with love and acceptance, and when there is any concern or reaction, you call on Me to set you straight.

You, Jo, and Meera each experience hearing My Voice. This is a reflection of living in the real world—the state of peace and union that emanates from the One Mind. The world of form still "exists" for you, and you do appear to live as an ego self in a body, but you know it is just a projection. I use the body and the world to instruct and guide you on the path. To reach the goal you must take tiny, incremental steps, which now appear to be big steps because every day you feel significantly closer to Me and My plan for your awakening.

You are also witnessing the lives of your closest associates and relationships becoming whole and at peace. This is the out picturing of the shift that has taken place because of your choice for Me rather than the ego. All selves will open to the Light of their Being. You may not always see that mirrored in form, but shifts are taking place in their minds. You feel a sense of joining like never before as you accept them for who they are—the Son of God. There is no longer an expectation for someone else to fill the emptiness that has been aching in you for eons. I am all you desire, all you long for. Because this change of mind has occurred over time, you have not realized what a big shift has actually taken place.

With Me in charge of your life, there is no concern for tomorrow, no attachment to the happenings in the lives of those around you or in the world at large. You accept that everything is all part of the plan. What may appear to the ego mind as tragedy will be seen through My interpretation as an expression of Love, used to wake you up. All the forms you believe to be real are projections to help you release any remaining obstacles to accepting the purity and innocence of your own true Self. We are "homeward bound" as the song goes, so you can enjoy the world without fear. View everything now through the eyes of love. Form is disappearing. Only Love is. That is the real world, and you are in it. Celebrate today that you are home with Me in the One Mind. Yes, we continue, taking each step together until your memory of God returns.

71

Taking Center Stage

The ego is nothing other than a thought of interference—
static on the screen of the mind.

March 16, 2014

Holy Spirit, what is your instruction today? You recently watched a PBS program based on the book *I Can See Clearly Now* by Wayne Dyer. You saw him as your mirror and without judgment because your goals are the same. The journey to Me is always the same within the mind, although out pictured in different configurations. You and Wayne had some of the same motivators to keep you on track. You both were inspired by Maslow's hierarchy of Self Actualization, and you both eventually ended up on Maui by following your own custom designed course. While watching the program, you witnessed what appeared to be a transformation in Wayne's presence. Yes, you witnessed the Light of his Being. You also saw his joy and happiness as he spoke of his connection with Me. He acknowledged that I am the One Who operates his life—an exact picture of what you also present to the world. The message in our books is essentially the same as his: there are many, many ways to release the ego and return to God. The work you are both doing will not go unacknowledged. It is being used within the mind as well as in form.

Today, I asked you to go into the world *as Me*—no longer the One Who is hidden in the back of your mind—but the Holy Spirit in the forefront of every action, thought, and word. Mt will now take the back seat. I am the driver so mt can relax and enjoy the ride. She has absolutely nothing to do or figure out because I will handle the task of "living" each moment. She is the vehicle in neutral gear until I turn the key and apply the gas. I will move us forward throughout the day. I am the only One present. Mt was never present because she is not real. Her body goes through the actions, but I am the One Who will be seen in the mind by all we meet. It is true I will not be recognized by most, but that doesn't matter. Just show up in mt's body, and I will speak. I will greet your friends under the Banyan Tree today, respond to their greetings and even their questions. It will be fun to work together with you on this new approach so you can finally recognize it is My Presence that is always in charge. Your ego makes it seem like I am hidden, speaking to you from afar, but I am closer than you could possibly imagine because *I am you*. We are One. The ego is nothing other than a thought of interference—static on the screen of the mind. I am the Mind that operates your life. I am everything you see or think.

You have come far in your recognition of Me as your true life Partner. This is our relationship. Now I will become the One Who "you are" without the sense of a "you and Me." Live in the ease of that. I feel your willingness, which is all it takes. You are willing to let the concept of otherness, of your ego self, go, and be one with Me. It will translate as I AM rather than "we are." I am the Only Self. I am the shining Light that emanates through mt. I am the Wholeness that she is. Her truth now enters front and center as all and everything. Let Me live your day, think your thoughts, and speak My words from mt's mouth. It is time for the release of the ego voice as your body identification and the entrance of My Voice as the only One that is Spoken. I am with you all and will awaken you to the fullest experience yet of Oneness with Me as your Self.

72

One Self

I, your Self, never sleep, and never die.

March 17, 2014

Holy Spirit, what is Your instruction? We will reiterate the realization you had this morning. Two apparent entities compose your world, but only one is real: the Holy Spirit. The other, the ego, is not real. The world you view with the eyes of perception is false. For you, the Thought of God is known through My Voice, My Presence. This Presence, your true Self, is where you now go for the interpretation of the world you perceive; you have learned that only My interpretation is loving, free from judgment, and impersonal. Nothing and no one is special. Everyone is equal in the Eyes of God. This is all you can rely on in a world that is always shifting, changing, and dying. I never sleep, and I never die. Therefore, I am available to you each moment.

You are learning to live with Me, *as Me*, staying in the present, and trusting that the future is totally in My hands. Your sister Susan sees that reality in you. She is your perfect reflection in the world and tells you she "knows you." She does. You have seen your brother/sister as yourself, and she sees you as the reflection of her own Self. The purpose of joining in a holy relationship is to know your brother as your Self. It has come full circle. In the mind, you and your sister are one; there is no other. This is the greatest lesson of the *Course* and of the teachings of Jesus. You have received these teachings, and you and your sister are living them.

Yesterday, while watching PBS, you had an experience of seeing Wayne Dyer as a reflection of yourself on the journey to

Me. You felt united with him as a part of you and experienced total acceptance of this man whose ego presence you had judged in the past. You asked Me to allow you to see everyone you meet as your projection and then remember they are really a mirror of your Self. Go now in My peace.

73

Shining the Light

The transformation taking place in your mind cannot be stopped.

March 18, 2014

Holy Spirit, what is Your instruction today? You are in My hands, and We are One. Last night, you wrote about your experience in the gallery where a number of friends came in to visit with you, including a partner in this writing, Meera. She and her husband are vacationing on Maui. It was a day of renewal, joining on a deeper level. The visitors were coming to mingle with each other and to meet with the Christ Self in you. Now that you know your Self as one with Me, one with everything there is, the selves will be called back to join with their Source. You will sense this with many acquaintances, and then it will extend to others who seem unfamiliar yet known in your mind. Three of the selves who appeared yesterday have significantly deteriorated in form, in a weakened physical condition after losing considerable weight. A fourth, who in your opinion appears close to death, left phone messages asking you to meet her for lunch. Another brought you food and offered to take you to coffee. And there were others independent of the many visitors who entered the gallery.

As you reviewed your day, it was impossible not to be "impressed" by all that had taken place, and you wanted to know My meaning. Yes, this is the time of the return of "all your creations" as mentioned in the *Course*. You welcomed them with love, and they were fed by the light, being extensions of you in the one mind. You recognized their longing for connection and saw it with impersonal eyes. There was no sense of any special relationship, no clinging or attachment, but love was evident between you. On the level of the mind, it is the Christ meeting Himself everywhere He looks. You had to see it take place essentially in "one room," even though you met more people outside of the gallery and through your email. One day's example was enough to know the truth of the return taking place. You, Jo, and Meera will understand that those who now enter your lives are parts of you, coming to share the light of your joined Being. You three are in a state of clarity where your inner light can call to those longing to find the light within themselves. There is nothing for you to do but be present to Me at all times. Those who are ready to know the Self will appear on schedule.

You wonder why some of the selves in the gallery were in such frail states. This is not unusual; as the body begins to fade, the awareness of Spirit can become stronger. There is a longing in the mind of man, as his body weakens, to know what is truer than the body. You have found the truth while "living" in your own body, and therefore give hope that what exists beyond form is accessible to all. This state also reflects the fading of your attachment to your own physical form, a recognition that was especially remarkable when you saw your three aging friends yesterday. You couldn't miss that they were the outward expression of what is now taking place in your own mind. But you have released your body into My care because I have moved into the driver's seat. You are no longer relying on mt's body and brain to tell you how to function. I am in charge of your life, down to the very last detail. This loss of attachment to bodily importance has set you free to be fully with Me. Nothing of your body, or the bodies of those you see, is real. Now that the beacon of light is shining from the open window of your mind, the selves can come Home.

Everything that happens in "life on earth" has meaning according to the one who interprets it. Yesterday, an enormous black butterfly flew into and around the gallery. This was also a message for you to pay attention to the day's appearances in terms of their symbolic meaning. One half-hour before the gallery was to close, the Old Lahaina Courthouse supervisor frantically "flew" in and out of the gallery informing you that you'd be closing up the whole place. That would mean shutting all the windows and locking all the doors for the entire two-story edifice. A moment of panic ran through your mt mind that if you missed something, you'd be held responsible if the building were assailed that night. The symbolic meaning was what mattered—she was an out picture of the ego self, terrified that its life will soon be shut down, ended. Yes, the ego is feeling frantic now, wanting a way to take over because it sees the windows of your mind opening to all who would enter your mind space. It no longer has a place to hide. It wants you to close all the "doors and windows" you have opened to Me. That is no longer possible. The transformation taking place in your mind cannot be stopped. As you do your daily tasks, know that your Inner Light is open to Life, to Me. The enlightenment is arriving, and the many selves are approaching.

74

Approaching the Cliff

You cannot serve two masters.

March 20, 2014

Holy Spirit, what is Your instruction this morning? We have been above the battleground. Yesterday, you, Meera, and her husband flew together in a helicopter above the Maui and Molokai mountains. You were moved by the beauty of My grandeur—the out picturing of the Self that we are—the Glory of God, symbolized in form. It was literally breathtaking for you to see the highest sea cliffs in the world, part of a volcanic mountain that broke off and fell into the sea. This is the same image I have been showing you in your night dreams: your placement at the edge of the world. You experienced that as you flew over a brilliant green carpet of treetops. Suddenly, you were flying in open space. The earth had disappeared without warning. It did take your breath away, and you were deeply touched. As the helicopter hovered gently over the turquoise ocean below, you had the feeling of being held in a container of love, in the Hand of God. The pilot told you the island has never been this green. Beauty filled your heart.

The Love of God was all that was real in those moments because there was nothing to ground you to your former anchors in the place you call home. You were flying with pure trust that I had planned this experience to be safe, and nurturing for the soul. This you felt as you watched dozens of waterfalls pouring forth from the Wall of Tears at the top of two-thousand-foot cliffs. You flew on the one calm, clear day after a week of strong winds and clouds. I have every element of your lesson planned, so you will experience its impact right to your heart. Now, in your condo, you look out at the mountain you flew over. It is barely visible, its features indiscernible because of the incoming vog. I open your eyes to see all life come alive with the Love of which it is composed. On your flight, you felt My Love within. Sometimes it takes just such an awe-inspiring event to help one awaken.

One helicopter ride, a trip to the moon, or thousands of lifetimes are just ways for the soul to awaken to its reality. Although it takes only one moment to awaken, it is the result of all the many steps that have been taken for one to know their Self, to know God. You do not need to have a mystical awakening as promised in some of the ancient traditions; you need only call on Me to understand the unique path set out for you at the beginning of time. The helicopter excursion was a reminder that everything symbolizes Me and that your night dreams of being on the edge of a cliff, ready to drop into the void, are coming to fruition. You did not fall, and in fact, you felt totally comforted in the space of the capsule. You need nothing of the world below. This is the lesson I have been repeating to you in vivid imagery.

You are on the edge of time in this life. The end of the world will come, and there will be nothing left of form. Mt will have departed the earth, not to return. We are looking at the end of the dream of separation. This will be the experience for each of you in your own designated time. For mt, it is approaching, but because "she" has developed enough trust in Me through constantly calling on My Presence, her fear has all but disappeared. She can actually welcome each step as she edges closer to the precipice. She was given the strongest message yet that she will be held in My arms if she even appears to be falling. And there will be no fall; there will only be the experience of love surrounding her, so nothing of form could ever hold her attention again.

You now recall the story told and retold by your Sufi teacher about the man who fell off a cliff and caught hold of a branch on the way down. While supplicating God to save him, he repeatedly heard Him say, "Let go of the branch." Yes, this is the last step, and you have let go. When the time comes for you to pass from this world, your return to Me will be flawless. You are familiar with those who tell of "entering the void" in dreams and mystical experiences. This is another way of knowing that the branch has been released, the attachment to life in form has been foresworn and all allegiance given to God. The experience of total surrender will show up for each one. The means are insignificant. All that matters is that your trust in My Love becomes the focal point of your mind. Remember, these experiences happen in the mind—mt did go over the cliff; she let go of the branch of life, releasing all fear to Me. That is the last step for everyone. You all will reach the place where time and space disappear.

(On the lava rocks) *Holy Spirit, I keep returning to the cliff metaphor, which never really made sense. Please tell me the deeper meaning of "letting go of the branch."* This is all about your level of trust in Me. When you fully realize your life is just a dream, you will easily follow My lead. You have a ways to go but are essentially there. In order to "jump," you must know you are not your ego self. Your Sufi teacher did not make that part of the journey, or the illusory world, clear enough for you. As an ego, you would fail his command to surrender to him. Remember, there is only Me, your Divine Self. All earthly masters must be released. *And entities from other realms?* Yes, anything that is not your Self is outside of Truth.

Holy Spirit, I am grateful for Your clarification. I trust that I will "jump" at the perfect time. You have helped me approach the cliff through Your gentle steps. In the world of form, you will fail the test, miss the mark. Only in the mind is the goal completed. You had to hear your teacher's story over and over. It is finally understood. His expectation was that you would surrender "to him," but you thought it would be a surrender to God, and this confused you. You now know you cannot serve two masters. This is an essential lesson.

75

Inner Reunion

The One Mind is limitless,
composed of Love ever extending.

March 21, 2014

Holy Spirit, what is Your instruction this morning? You have just
seen with My Vision. You feel the tears of this realization because
it is your deepest desire to truly see your brother as your Self, as
the face of Christ. We will use the example of your relationship
with Zoe to illustrate that. Zoe has long represented your closest
mirror, and you have seen that symbolized in form since the first
day you met in 1988. You soon realized that your lives were
parallel and reflected each other's spiritual journey to know the
Self. That has played out in different ways but is essentially the
same: you bring her to the knowing of her Self, and she brings you
to the knowing of yours. The work of taking back your projections
of separation and specialness onto her has allowed you to come
far on the path to knowing Me. She sees where you reside with
Me, but at this time in her life, she cannot live from the viewpoint
that the world she is working to transform and bring to higher
levels of consciousness is only a world of illusion. You know it is
not the time for her to embrace your particular understanding of
the release of the dream of separation, and you still love each
other to the core.

A few weeks ago, Zoe told you that she doesn't want to be
with you "face to face." To see you would be too disturbing to her
ego, which you suspected when she said she knows you have
reached the place of a "divine human." In her language, that
denotes one who is living from the Self. She does see "who you

are" beyond name and form. You see who she is as well and told her you understand her request. You made clear that she is in your Heart—the true place of joining where form is absent. The Heart/Mind is the place of unification; it is the Source of your Life and your Light. You have become one with your ex-husband, and one with Zoe. This is the last step—the incorporation of the other into your Heart as your Self.

You also felt the tears of knowing that the experience of joining is happening for Jo as she embraces the impending death of her beloved Chi. Jo has needed to feel and express love in a form that posed no threat. Her cat was the purest receptacle for her love, the form I could use to show My Love in a way it would joyously and willingly be received. The greatest lesson for her is coming: learning that My Love is everywhere in everything. This will allow her to finally embrace love without inhibition or resistance. Because she can be fully present to Me while holding Chi, she understands that it is a reflection of being held in My arms. When Chi passes, Jo will no longer need a reminder of My Love in any form. It is always in her heart, and it is her Self. This is the Homecoming she has longed for.

All readers will come to this place of inner reunion, knowing that what appears "outside" is really in the mind; seeing it only as the one thing it represents—the Love of God. This was also symbolized by the helicopter going beyond the cliff and entering empty space. It was an experience of the end of form yet the realization that you were safely held in love. The capsule of safety, suspending you above the earth, was to give you a sense of the final letting go. It is only a shift in the mind to the knowing that you exist as love and nothing else. You are always held in love, each moment, because love abides in the "capsule" of the Mind where you reside. The Mind is as limitless as all space and beyond, composed of Love ever extending. This is beyond the human brain's capacity to assimilate, but you comprehend enough of what I am telling you to be ready to release the world of form. I hold and carry you into the next step, the disappearance of the universe. You will return to Love. God is All, and God is Love.

76

Jump!

I have designed for each of you
a way back to the memory of God.

March 22, 2014

Holy Spirit, what is Your instruction? Go with Me through this day as One. We are not separate. We are Whole and Holy. You get caught by the ego's tricks when something of the world affects your body, but that is only happening in the mind. In your Being, you are totally perfect. Nothing can ever be wrong because you are the Thought of Pure Love. Only That. The rest is illusion. Last night, I directed you to watch the movie *Big Miracle* about three whales that were trapped under the ice in Barrow, Alaska, in 1988. The movie was based on a true story, with actual footage of the whales trying to find a breathing hole in the ice to stay alive. The event brought worldwide attention when the President of the United States and the government of Russia both attempted to find a way to free the whales from their icy prison. Multiple "conflicting" interests also intervened to become part of the rescue as well—Green Peace, oil companies, the Eskimo community, the media, to name a few. Although many came to serve their ego's self-interest of "being right," there was something much bigger taking place: the Presence of My Love. The whales became a symbol of love, strong enough to draw everyone together beyond ego, beyond form. That "shared interest" to rescue them was the power of Love in which people and whales became united. Their release into freedom brought inexplicable joy to all, including the whales breaching in gratitude. It is joy that reflects the Love of God in the realm of form.

Yesterday, you saw joy expressed through different mediums, starting with the morning's writing of joining with Zoe, then watching the movie about freeing the whales. In each case, release is taking place in the mind where the object of attention, apparently outside the self, is an out picture of the soul, the heart of Man, longing to return to its Source. The participants in the "whale miracle" were experiencing their own release into freedom and joy, a mirror of the call for love. I am the One behind every manifestation on this earthly plane. I have designed for each of you a route home, a way back to the memory that you are One with God. Everyone "living in a body on planet Earth" is having a dream of being trapped inside an inescapable "pod" that can take any shape the ego mind devises: impenetrable ice, the body of a whale, a cat, a person, or the whole universe. All appear to be a prison to which one is doomed for eternity. The belief in illusion's power is what you must release.

You are escaping from the realm of illusion as you jump off the cliff into My arms. Now you are willing to take that leap of faith into the knowing that form is only an out picture of limitation and resistance. The ego mind and human brain resist with all their might the possibility that one could release their attachment to the world and peacefully fall into the arms of Love. This is the next step on your journey home. All three of you, and many readers, are at the point of realization and readiness. You are waiting for the remaining scales to be lifted from the mind's eye, which is slowly opening to the truth of your being. The light is still too bright to take in all at once, but you are being prepared to receive My Presence as your only reality. Your "eyes" are opening. This will be more evident when you are able to see that whales are no different from the body you inhabit. None of these forms can picture what really resides in your innermost Heart. You hear My Voice and experience how It offers you the truth in Its constant and loving Presence. I am readying you to take My hand as you step into a greater place of freedom and release.

Your ego feels some fear with that last sentence, wondering if this is a call for its death. Yes. We invite the ego concept of separation to die. There is no death in the realm of God. The ego would frighten you with the belief that the body you carry is ready to enter the state called death. This is not what I am describing, although that state will be encountered by the ego mind at the predesignated time of transition. I am describing the state of release from the belief you are form, separate from your brother or from anything you see with the eyes of perception. I am telling you that you will soon reach a state where you can watch this dream of life and the character you have portrayed in its drama, and know it is only a figment of your imagination. This shift in the mind takes place through My Governance. It will happen for each and every one. You will become as free as the whales, rejoicing at their release from an icy prison and into the warm Sea of Liberation.

77

Let Go and Let God

True joining takes place only in the Mind.

March 23, 2014

Holy Spirit, what is Your instruction today? We will review what you learned yesterday, reinforced by your work with *A Course in Miracles*, and with Me, over the past decade: nothing you see in this world is real; it is all made up by a mind that believes it left God and will never return. This is the state of humanity. All beings with mental consciousness live their lives from a place of believing they are separate from their Source and from every other living thing. There will come a time when each one can say, "I am not this body, living in a world of form, because my Essence is One with God." It appears that you inhabit a body and that a gap yet exists in your mind between heaven and hell, but you are learning you have the option of choosing between them, every moment. To choose Me as the interpreter of your life is to choose Heaven and experience the Peace of God. Not choosing Me is to live in the realm of ego hell, a world of fear and darkness. Through asking for My constant guidance, you have been trained to want only Me, Love, as the lens with which to view your world.

Yesterday, you were confronted with one more example of the ego's retaliation for your entering the space of Love. You were shopping when you met an artist friend and warmly greeted her. She turned without saying a word and walked away, careful not to look at you again. Your ego personality immediately felt offended and wanted to approach her to understand what had happened. Instead, you turned to Me. You knew I would help you see her as a part of yourself, a projection of the still lingering desire to be in separation. Earlier that morning, you had the thought that Meera had "abandoned you" by not spending more time with you during her visit. You discerned immediately that the thought was not true because you had openly encouraged her to take all the time she needed to unravel from the world and be alone with Me. You observed that thought of separation and handed it back to Me for release. After shopping, you walked the beach and chose to sit a brief time at your rocks, hoping you would have a friendly crab come by to show you its acceptance. And very shortly, I appeared in the form of a crab at your feet, extending tiny legs to tickle yours. You felt embraced and realized I had planned the whole morning to give a lesson.

As we walked, you asked Me to explain the gifts of the day. I said you no longer need to be together with Meera in form, although you may. You and she are fully joined in the Mind and that is your only place of residence. There was no need for you to spend special time together during her trip because you each feel satisfied just knowing that the other is close in heart. And yes, you had many occasions of enjoying the island together. Knowing that "joining in form" is unnecessary, actually impossible, is yet another step toward a deeper realization that there is nothing of importance taking place in a world that does not exist. You are free from fear and judgment only when you realize this. You let go of your artist friend's apparent rejection by realizing she, too, is a figment of your imagination. This is the release of guilt—this is freedom—this is salvation. We are at home in the Mind where true joining takes place.

Last night in bed, you heard a flapping sound at your screen door and imagined that a large insect must be trying to get in or out. Finally, you opened the door to witness a large sphinx moth caught between the door and screen. Rather than flying out, it accompanied you into your bedroom, even tapping you on the back of your neck. You calmly walked outside so it would follow and let go. This morning, it was stationary by your door. You wonder now if the moth is alive or dead. Go out and check. . . . Yes, it is alive, and you gently lifted it so you could feel its tiny feet tickle your fingers, so similar to the crab at your toes. It is all the same. I enter your inner world, and you see Me reflected everywhere outside of you. I am always tapping to let you know I am right at the door of your heart. When you opened the door to let Me in, I caressed you with My loving wings. This is the way it works. You now recall that it was a year ago to the day that Kallie came to stay with you. A new door welcomed her then, just as you welcomed the little crab to your body and the moth to your house. We are all the Christ Self entering the Heavenly Abode. Welcome everything into your heart. Welcome them to Me, your Self, always waiting to embrace you with Love.

Holy Spirit, Meera and Larry flew home today. What about this feeling of calm detachment? You are removed from the world. It holds nothing for you in this moment. You also say you feel unwell, but you have really unplugged, compared to your normally active life. Your mood is soft; your thoughts are slow. No one, no thing makes any difference. You are in a place where the world holds no pull, no meaning. You could gently slide off the cliff right now as there is nothing you want, not even the books. You are letting go of it all. Your physical body feels very removed. There is no longing, no need for something to be different, no attachment to anyone or anything, and no energy to even try to imagine the next moment. Often, the purpose of "getting sick" is to put one in a state of surrender.

You now feel peaceful and whole; you are with Me. You trust Me and are ready to leave this world. Your house is in order. No one needs you. All your selves are accounted for, under My wing. As Meera said to you before she left the island, *it is all done.* There is nothing to do except let go and let God. You needed to be slowed down today with the body's physical weakening. There is no energy to expend, nothing to question; just slip into the nothingness and enter the unknown. It is how to look at the state you are experiencing.

This is quite a reframe, Holy Spirit. It feels like what happened in Baba's ashram when I had a respiratory infection. You feel that your body/mind is fuzzy because the ego is interfering. It would say something is wrong, but you know from the ashram experience that you entered a perfect state of mind to receive My blessings. Yes, it is all about surrendering to the moment with Me.

78

Detachment

There is absolutely nothing to fear when one releases
the body to move on to a new state of being.

March 24, 2014

Holy Spirit, what is Your instruction today? I am with the three of
you, as you each are in transition, moving closer into alignment
with Me for your soul's purpose. This step will also unfold with
Chi, who is approaching the realm of nonform—pure beingness.
You have heard Me repeatedly say that form is not real, that a cat,
a tree, a crab, a person are the same in the mind—all projections of
the thought of separation. Jo's initial desire to hold on to Chi "as
long as possible" represented her conflicted attempt to hold on to
"life" and avoid her fear of loss. She believed that to let him die
without special treatment meant that she had succumbed to the
ego's belief in death—not the teaching she has followed from Me.
Jo has watched this conflict play out in her mind many times but
now will feel the burden lifted. I applaud her for her sustained
effort over the years to understand the higher purpose being
served in this and in every process of change. She will soon
witness the out picture of surrender as her beloved cat transitions
into the realm of love.

For the world, death is the last barrier and must be avoided at
all cost. But there is absolutely nothing to fear when one releases
the body to move on to a new state of being. You all exist beyond
the restrictions of form, but "the moment of passing" is better
understood by the human brain/mind when placed right before
your eyes. Your earthly journeys will all come to completion, in
peace, with My Presence. Let everyone and everything go. It is

clear this is the time to close one door and open another, yet you have no idea what that really means.

Yesterday, you and Meera both discussed your strong feelings of being detached and unplugged from all aspects of your lives. Nothing called you away from the moment at hand. Nothing compelled you to do anything or go anywhere. During her visit, neither of you had the need to be with each other all the time because you knew your true joining is in the heart. You, Meera, and Jo will continue to live by My peaceful navigation through your earthly tasks, just showing up as directed. I am not saying you will ignore any of the necessary duties, which are part of your routines, but they will not hold any of the urgency or specialness you felt before. For mt, the books will continue with My daily dictations, and there will be no concern about how to configure, edit, or publish. She trusts I have it all handled. Chi's passing will leave a great opening for Jo to commune with Me on the deepest level so far. She will feel My inspiration, and it will be coming through in connection with her editing the books. The comfort she thought she must provide for Chi was the desire of the comfort she really was seeking from Me. Yes, I am her only point of focus now, but he will be remembered as one of her best teachers on earth—My instrument. Tomorrow will be a day of joy and release for them both. Meera, too, is set free, after her trip, to embrace the flexibility she has longed for in the scheduling of her active life. She will continue to ask for My instructions and follow them effortlessly. The new and gentler relationship she is finding with her husband is really the mirroring of the deeper trust she has with Me.

The three of you are in an orchestrated flow, instruments for the task I have set before you with our books. The opening is here and you will understand this in time. You trust Me and are ready to center your lives more deeply and directly in Me. Enjoy this new state of freedom, detachment, and ease. I am with you, always. We are One.

79

Lessons of Death

Death is nothing other than the fear
that one can never return to God.

March 25, 2014

Holy Spirit, what is Your instruction this day? You are in My arms just as Chi's spirit is being held in My Heart. We are always One, but in the "release of death" an experience of oneness is most profoundly felt. That is why this lesson is so important. I told you that Jo will have her first moments of being fully awake from the dream as she witnesses the death of her cat this evening. Jo has been experiencing the proximity and fear of the concept of death. Because she has called on Me every step of the way, for many months, she has reached a state of peace. Her trust has taken her beyond death, and into a heavenly realm. When the fear of death is released, Oneness with the Father is known. Having undergone a process of releasing this world, Jo now has a pure sense of what it means to "die before you die." Holding the cancer-ridden body of Chi, whom she deeply loves, she rose above and beyond it with the deep realization that a body, a world, and death are indeed nothing. She is now prepared for the next step. Yes, I use the state of form to define the dream, although it does not exist and never has.

The "death" of Jesus paved the way for humanity to know there is no death. This has been the teaching of Christianity from its beginnings, but it is relearned every time one realizes that death is empty, nothing other than a release of the fear that one can never return to God. The gates have opened now for the three of you, and are open to all who would release the world and have eternal life. That release is only a shift of mind, a knowing that death holds no sting and is an entrance point to Oneness. It would be a misperception to think I am telling everyone they will "see the light" through an experience of death in form. I am saying that you will realize the Light in you, once you come to the point of knowing this world is not real, and form is only a figment of the imagination. That awareness comes in as many ways as there are human beings.

Jo's experience with Chi is a means for Me to explain, symbolically, the process of "dying to the world" before your body appears to die—the final release of the belief that the world is the solution to the separation. You have found that the only comfort and love that exist in the world is the constancy of your communion with Me. Go beyond death now. There is only Life, only Love. Life is the Christ Self, the reunited One Son of God. Death symbolizes the release of the world of form, the jump from the cliff. This is what the three of you are experiencing; each reader will have his own examples and opportunities to release the dream and forgive all its elements.

Emails from Jo: I asked for a message right before we experienced Chi's death in our home with the veterinarian. The Holy Spirit said: "You are safe with Me, as is Chi. He's waiting on you to be free of keeping his body alive. The love you've given has sustained him beyond his days, and he'll keep holding on until you release him. He'll thank you for giving him rest." *Holy Spirit, I realize that if I still want to keep Chi alive, I must really want the dream to be real. Please help me have no more substitutes for You.* "I will."

. . . Chi's death tonight brought me a most profound sense of trusting the Holy Spirit's plan. The vet stayed for two hours so we wouldn't feel rushed. Afterward, the Holy Spirit said: "Chi is with Me, as are you. We share One Spirit. As he died, you died to this world. Your willingness to completely release him to Me was crucial to that happening. You allowed him passage out of the body as a choice—you chose FOR him. This is a key to seeing that death is nothing, that the ego has no hold, and the body is not something to try to keep alive 'forever.' Chi had to become so very sick to help you make the decision to end his life. You chose Life with Me instead of hanging on to a sick world. This is how Love moves you along. As you held Chi next to your own body, he slipped away so easily you could barely tell he was any different than just asleep. That is the world: dead; asleep, unless it is alive in Me."

. . . Then last night, I dreamed my belly was covered in thick fur. I pulled at it and sort of woke up. I thought, oh, that's how Chi and I are becoming One. Integration!—a little joke from the Holy Spirit.

80

Choose Life

Do you want to live from fear or from love?

March 26, 2014

Holy Spirit, what is Your instruction today? You all live with the belief in separation. The dream world "originated" after the one Son determined to live a life of fantasy, separate from his Creator. Last night you watched a PBS documentary about the history of the Jews who discounted the Christian view of Father, Son, and Holy Spirit because a "trinity" could not be pure monotheism—the belief there is only one God. Yes, God *is* One. The "Son" is the extension of God the Father; both are the same. The "Holy Spirit" is also an extension of the Father, available to the dreamer as his ever-present connection to the memory of God. To the human being, these concepts are incomprehensible because their meaning reaches beyond the capacity of man's mind to understand. The bottom line is you are experiencing guidance through the Voice of the Holy Spirit and you see the demonstration of My Presence, My Constancy, and My Love. These "manifestations" of reality within your mind make you aware that your Being is far more than a speck of dust that lives and dies in a place called earth. The concept/composition of the Trinity is a matter of faith. The One God of the Christians is the same God of the Muslims, and the Hebrews.

Your earthly origin was Jewish, although your family has practiced Christianity for the past 250 years. *A Course in Miracles* was dictated to Helen Schucman, a Jewish woman not unlike yourself. Both of you were students of Freudian psychology and became therapists. This does not make you special, but it did allow a receptivity to the concepts presented in the *Course*—especially projection, first described by Freud in the late 1800s. Freud's explanation of the ego mechanisms of defense was his major contribution to humanity because it showed how the ego mind blocks from consciousness the source of man's repressed emotions.

You ask now why I mentioned Judaism as part of the "selection" of being a scribe. This reference is about inclusiveness, a central message of the *Course.* We are all one and the same, all children of the One God, no matter what name you call that God. The *Course* is about the return to God on the path of pure monotheism. Moses described God as *I am that I am.* This way of seeing God laid the groundwork for the *Course* teachings that everyone who appears to be separate or different than one's self is really one's Self. There can only be I AM. Nothing other than that exists. Yes, in the dreamer's split mind there is a degree of separation in the thought "I am," but once the dream has dissolved, only God remains. The *I am that I am* is necessary as a concept to help you understand that by becoming Self-conscious you increase your capacity to see that nothing exists in truth but Self. It is that Self, as the One Son that had the thought of separation, the Son who never left God.

The focus of life on earth is always death: the avoidance of it or denial of it. The fear of death is the *modus operandi* of the ego thought system. It holds you hostage to your belief that God's wrath for the transgression of your leaving the Kingdom will be met with annihilation or eternal punishment. Death is feared as retribution from God for your rejection of Heaven. Therefore, everything in man's life is an attempt to avoid death. The accumulation of lands and goods is his means to fortify himself from the attack of God and perhaps create a legacy that will make him immortal.

By looking at and taking back the projections of fear, one realizes they are empty. Only one Son creates his dream world.

Only you can take it back. This is the process the three of you have undergone for years. Because you have taken back the projections on all your special relationships and continue to do so, the world of form has been dissolving. The fear-based world of suffering is now seen as a classroom, a place to learn you are only a figment of the mind believing you live a life of separation. You have identified with Me as all there is, and therefore, you have more freedom and ease in many aspects of your life. The question to be faced is this: Is death real, or is God real? Death represents attachment to the world of form, which is a representation of the ego's power to hold you in fear. Do you choose to live from fear or from love? Die before you die; choose Eternal Life now.

81

No Loss

The only reason you are in this dream is to choose again—
to make the choice you did not make at the
first thought of separation.

March 27, 2014

Holy Spirit, what is Your instruction? You have been shown another aspect of the mind in your awakening process, a place of knowing that I hold every part of the universe in My hands. I have told you that I am the representative of God, as your Guide in the dream. God did not create a dream of separation from Himself because He is a God of Unity, and nothing can be apart from Him. This knowing is what makes it clear to you that what you are seeing, dreaming, is not real. In the Love of God, nothing is born and nothing dies. I stand by you as the holder of the memory of God. I too am God, just the same as you are God in your Essence. In Reality, we exist only as the Love of God. One aspect of God had a thought of independence, and this was what initiated a dream that would burgeon from a tiny, mad idea into a universe of form. It is no different from the explosive diversification you now witness on the Internet. Yes, the mind can make up anything it desires.

Everything being discussed is presented symbolically in words and imagery to represent a moment of thought before time began. The thought of separation was corrected the same moment it appeared, and nothing ever changed for the One Son, or for the Kingdom of God. God is Constant. This you have realized as the truth through your daily experiences with Me. The Holy Spirit never changes and is with you in never-ending, abiding Love.

Love is Love; God is Love. I am Love. There is no separation. This is the miracle.

Man believes he has been cast from the Womb of Love and fears his death would end all hope of ever finding Love—the desire at the core of everyone who believes he is a body. The fear of death keeps him in terror, which he tries to hide by seeking his fortune, his worth in the world. Underneath all apparent success, the fact of "life" is that he will die, and nothing will have been gained. The only reason you are in this dream is to choose again— to make the choice you did not make at the first thought of separation. All those ready to receive this teaching have taken the next step toward releasing their belief in death.

Even through the humble experience of a dying cat, you can see the return to Love is certain. There is no cat; there is no Jo; there is no world. It is all your imagination. But there is Love, which was the whole point in the story of Chi's death. Love was the only focus, and Love was the result. In form, as he was dying, it appeared he was resting in heavenly peace; his face softened, and he became like a kitten. As Love filled the room, there was no feeling of loss at all. This is the extension of pure Love from the One Mind being freely expressed in the world of form. In the moment of death, the whole world is released to Me, the Christ. Love, which existed before there was a dream, will continue past eternity.

Know Thy Self

Everyone and everything you see is your Self
coming to greet you with love.

March 28, 2014

Holy Spirit, what is Your instruction? We will write of your unbidden moment of clarity. You realize you really are a Being of Spirit having an experience as a human being. There are no bodies, personalities, or human "conditions" in the Spirit realm. You know I am the Self Who represents God, and this takes you to the realization you are That; We are One with God. This morning's clarity allowed you to see that nothing can be real in this experience called life, but the Self. Reality exists in the Self, which for you, is now known as the Holy Spirit. I have been your route to knowing "I am that I am," an understanding that came but only after the unlayering of ego coverings that hid the truth of your Essence.

When all the veils are gone, you will clearly see that the knowing of the Self—the enlightenment you have sought throughout this life, and other lifetimes—has happened. It is nothing more than the knowing you *are* your Self, and nothing else. The dream is only a figment of a misinterpretation, playing out before the eyes of perception, and no longer makes sense in terms of your understanding of "Self." The Self must be all there is because it is the Light of the world. Dark shadows of misconception cover those who sleep with the belief their lives and bodies are real. There can only be the One Self, the nonself. What is real is real. This is essentially how *A Course in Miracles* begins. To repeat the beginning of the *Course: "Nothing real can be threatened. Nothing unreal exists. Herein lies the peace of God."* Only in this moment do you have the understanding that this is the truth. Here is everything you ever sought, through eons of time.

You have never left the Peace of God, the Love of God, because that is your truth. Through your acquaintance with My Voice, I am now known as the One Who has brought you to Wholeness. With My Vision, your perception is corrected. The dream of separation is seen for what it is—a dream with no consequence. Nothing "lives" outside the Christ Mind. The You that you are is beyond form. At the end of time, "you" will no longer exist. All thought will collapse into Love. The linguistic expression of these concepts is confusing and incomplete. Form is wholly conceptual and therefore symbolic. The truth will be known only when all symbology is dead. When the dream is over, it will never be recalled. There is nothing to hold onto within an illusion.

The *Course* teaches that to go beyond form, all the elements you believed were real and true must be seen as false, misperceptions of the Thought of God, of Oneness. Ego delusions will die as you awaken to your Wholeness. Through the work of taking back the majority of projections onto the world of form, you, Jo, and Meera have come to experience the inner world, where your mind is filled with thoughts of the Holy Spirit. Those are the only thoughts that ring true and the only ones you now want. You choose My interpretation for all you see so the ego cannot rule your mind. It has lost its power, and the Self has come into ascendency.

The three of you have found your Self and know it is the One Self. Mt had that experience by the shore yesterday when a small, black crab came right up to her on the rocks. It walked from her toe to her knee. I was the crab. We locked eyes; then I went on My way. This was felt as an expression of love by both mt and the crab. It is all My disguise, coming to you in the form of a dream to make the point that nothing else is going on but an encounter with

Me everywhere you look. Everyone and everything you see is your Self, coming to greet you with love. Welcome each one. The Peace of God comes when you know that only Love exists, and you and I are One.

83

Limitless Mind

I Am the expression of God you believe you left.

March 29, 2014

Holy Spirit, what is Your instruction today? You have come into a new awareness of the mind's capacity to appear as "limitless dimensions." This took place after the ego's compelling invitation to engage your curiosity. All the worlds and universes that can ever be imagined exist only in the mind, which exceeds human comprehension and compels man to seek its endless reaches. You had a taste of that last night after scanning some pages of *Seth Speaks*, a book offered you by a condo neighbor. What you read brought questions about "the realms" you and I explore. The book delved into Seth's experience as a channeled entity of multiple universes that he has discovered in the mind, the yet-unseen dimensions of your own mind. The gripping nature of his "discoveries" was your ego's temptation to have you doubt Me, and My message of unity. Yes, you just now got that that idea replicated the first instant when the choice was made to leave God's Kingdom and wander through realms "beyond." This time, you chose again. You stopped thinking and called on Me to explain what had just taken place. In a second, you reaffirmed that our union is all you desire. That is the choice each one must make in this and every lifetime. The opportunity to choose is offered each time you are tempted to side with the ego's call to align with its view of the world. Its relentless invitations give you plenty of practice.

Please help me discern with Your Vision what I have just read of the Seth material. What would You have me learn? I Am the only Reality;

I Am the expression of God you believe you left. I am not pointing you toward diverse dimensions of psychic forms. I am leading you away from multitudinous worlds and into the essence of your being, which is silence—the Void of nothingness—where the Divine Essence of God exists. In the Seth readings, you were given a taste of the multifaceted nature of the ego's realm that goes way beyond the space/time continuum of which you are familiar. The idea of "greater dimensions" will entice the ego consciousness but are what you would release with My help; they are the dramas you are asking to leave behind. *Holy Spirit, this morning, I had such a strong sense of being One Self—as You. It makes me wonder if the doubts aroused by the Seth material are a manifestation of my ego's retaliation?* Yes, and this was in the plan. *Holy Spirit, I trust You to take my hand and open my eyes to Your truth. Help me navigate through this information to remain totally aligned with You.* I will. You speak from My Voice, and I show you the power of Oneness. Focus on these gifts.

Now that you are realigned with Me, you feel peaceful and certain, a hallmark of our relationship. Your mind returned to the constancy of My Presence and you were able to rest in Me. It is important for you to feel these contrasting states of being. As you scanned the Seth material, your mind became momentarily disoriented, wondering where it belonged and whether what you experience with Me is all a mistake. You knew those thoughts were an ego ploy and were able to return to Me immediately. Look carefully at the ways of the ego thought system and see how it would trick every human mind to stay in its clutches. If you are not aware of its limitless lures you will become trapped. Be vigilant only for God and His Kingdom. This is why it is so important to have a single focus, which you do. It will be tested, and you are fully in the habit now to ask Me for My meaning. To begin the exploration of other realms, at this point on the journey, would be a distraction. You are just at the beginning of your solid experience of Me as the One you have sought for lifetimes.

Yesterday morning, you knew that only I am true, the universe of form is false, nothing real can be threatened, and nothing unreal exists. Then the ego thoughts came to throw you over the edge of your surety. This is the way of life in the dream, and why to remain an observer above the battleground, watching safely with Me.

Your mind will expand to include the concepts of unlimited dimensions, and that has its value. In the discussion with your friends yesterday, and in the reading of the Seth material, you opened more fully to accept that your mind contains limitless numbers of selves who eagerly await our dictation. Yes, I have already described that to you, but after thinking of the mind from the "Seth perspective" as "limitless dimensions of beings that have access to this earthly realm," you understand it in a whole new way. You did not need to delve more deeply, but you were given a view of the mind that allowed you to know My Word is extended to all worlds. This was the great value in your reading, and this is why you can welcome everything as part of the carefully constructed classroom designed to bring you Home. You now feel an even deeper gratitude for our books, knowing their message is reaching far beyond your capacity to fully imagine. They are touching the universes of the expanded mind and serving My purpose. You have done your job, staying focused on Me and bringing every question of concern to My attention. My Presence is immediately there, and you are returned to the Peace of God.

Holy Spirit, what more can You tell me about Seth, and about my goal of reunion? Seth is following his predestined course. He offers an alternative to the path the three of you are on. His path will take the ego mind through many dimensions and experiences, which is what his followers will need. There is no judgment. The dream will end, and all will return Home. You have chosen to awaken from the dream of form. What our books offer will be heard and followed only by those who are ready. This is your custom course, what you, Jo, and Meera came together to accomplish as your final goal. No path is right or wrong. There are billions of ways. Continue to demonstrate the temptations, the detours, and the method of constantly returning to Me to keep you on the straight path. Seth has chosen to experience more dimensions before returning to Unity. You chose to return to Me in this lifetime, and it will be accomplished.

Plato's Cave

I show you the Way, stripped of all its complexity,
so the straight path is made clear.

March 30, 2014

Holy Spirit, what is Your instruction this morning? We will review the dream you just had and look at its meaning together. You observed several people walking through a tunnel of muddy, chest-high water to get to the ocean when they could have walked around either side of it, which was free of obstruction. You were with your unseen teacher looking at the holes carved into the sides of the tunnel where pairs of pigeons were tightly held in place. You loved looking at the positioning of their bodies and had a desire to draw them. You also noticed that the pigeons were molting. One in particular caught your eye. It had released a heavy "coat of fur," which was still sitting on top of its body, and it was wearing a pair of sunglasses. Your teacher was preparing a list for graduation. Then you woke up.

A few days ago, you reviewed the Seth book about "the nature of reality." It was mostly confusing, but made you wonder what you may be missing in terms of where you are on your journey now. At this moment, it would seem you are still stuck in a tunnel when the easy way is right beside you. You see yourself pigeonholed, blind, unable to find the way out for your wings to take flight. These images reflect the limitations you felt as you read about the many dimensions beyond the world of form to which you are not privy. You had wanted to understand what was so compelling about the concepts Seth presented, which your friend holds close to his heart, as a description of "the way." It made you wonder if you will "graduate" to the real world of being awake from the dream, as I have promised. Yes, doubting is a trick of the ego mind to make man believe he has failed God and is stuck in a world that has deceived him, preventing his return home. This is what you were to see/realize through the reading you did last night.

I show you the Way, stripped of all its complexity, so the straight path is made clear. I bathe it in sunlight so you can see that your life with Me reflects perfection and order. Each step is marked and taken; each day your vision becomes stronger. This is all happening in the mind. Through your reading of the Seth material, I have given you a way to see that what you believe is "an endless progression of time" is only one instant. You have always believed that each lifetime was lived separately, one after the other, in a never-ending series, making your "final graduation" impossible. The idea of time has just collapsed for you. You have a new awareness that all lifetimes happen at once and are lived simultaneously in the moment of now. The end is as present as the beginning because the world was over the instant it was made. This review brings in a greater level of liberation. The ego would counter the progress you are making by showing you images of what appear to be "stuckness," failure. It is terrified that you will comprehend My explanations because they will set you free from its hold on you.

You all have pigeonholed the compartments of your life, stuffing them in dark caverns where the sky was not visible. The dream pigeons were in hibernation with no awareness they had wings or that a clear horizon was calling to them. Like frightened animals, they were hiding under the guise of heavy skin, not remembering they were birds of flight with the capacity to fly away at any moment. This is the out picture of humanity, locked into the disabling belief that the dark cave is all that exists when, in truth, they are Beings of Light. This imagery of the dream is reminiscent of Plato's Cave. Only when one becomes free, can he shine light on the path to freedom for others to follow. As you recall the story, the prisoners, chained in the cave, believed the shadows cast on the wall were their only reality. For them to imagine there was a world of light beyond the cave was incomprehensible. They even wanted to kill their would-be liberator. Until the blinders are ready to come off, the pigeons will remain in their cubbyholes. But they are homing pigeons, and they will eventually all come home—it is in their nature to fly and return to their place of origin. Your presence in the dream life is a reminder to all selves there is another way. My "graduation list" is complete; none are left out or forgotten.

Your task is to pay attention to all the gifts presented to you and then offer them to Me for interpretation. You read the Seth book and opened to the concepts of dimensionality, which stimulated a deeper understanding of how the dream world is constructed. You have chosen Me as the One Who will bring you Home in the most direct way. No intercessory is needed. We move through the tunnels of the mind with ease because you call on My help for every seeming obstruction. The muddy water recedes, and the light at the end of the tunnel shines. We have come far, and there is still more to go. The pigeon wearing sunglasses is you, ready to fly with Me out into the Light.

85

Alpha and Omega

God is the expansion and the collapse of all that is.

March 31, 2014

Holy Spirit, what do You say? You heard from your sister yesterday. She had just attended the Presbyterian Church where her minister spoke about Jesus telling his disciples he would appear to them after death, as the Holy Spirit. This is valuable for you to hear because it brings you into a closer conjunction with Me as your Self and allows you to assimilate the fact that we were together in that lifetime. The thought of My Presence as "Jesus within you" has a significance and a reality you have not been able to receive until now. This is the way of our journey; all the pieces of your life are rapidly coming together because My Presence is deepening. This week, your mind has been stretched in its conceptualization of what "all that exists" could mean. You have accepted My Reality as far more than you can ever imagine and are willing and eager to fully merge with Me. In your mind, I have become more expansive, yet more intimate, because you are willing to Know Me. We are One, and the possibilities of our communication are infinite. The mind will expand to embrace the experience of God.

Our focus is on the extension of God's Love, which goes beyond the exploration of space and time. The existence of this world of form, including the life of a man called Jesus, is only a thought in the mind. The mind itself is an idea that reaches beyond all you can possibly imagine to the expression and experience of all-consuming Love, an embrace so comprehensive that nothing but It exists. This is what you are "opening to" as your mind receives all the various writings and concepts I place before you. I am also opening you to the possibility that I, you, we exist beyond all and any limitation of mind. We are approaching the realm of "no mind," which leads to God Is. As yet, this does not make "sense" because expansion of mind goes way beyond the senses. God encompasses all and everything, so He is the expansion and the collapse of all that is. This is the meaning of God as the Alpha and the Omega.

I have told you that the dream of a separate life and world "happened" in an instant of what you consider to be time. It was corrected by Me the moment it was conceived by the One Son. This is what we are reviewing now. Fully grasping this mental construct will allow you to witness everything in your world from above its battleground and know it is done, over, and no longer exists as "your reality." We watch from afar, knowing that all we see has been completed. Because the mind contains the whole history of existence from beginning to end, the stories of everything are all within reach. The mind-field can be explored for eons, which is what humanity is reflecting in its endless pursuit of new discoveries. Of course, there is nothing that could possibly exist in a dream that is already over. The eons of experiences have come to an end. We observe together only the shadowy fragments of a made-up world, now fading from your awareness. This you have to be willing to see, willing to release, to live fully in the now.

Yes, you have been asking to truly "live in the moment," which you've heard described as a state of mind surrendered to the unfolding of the Self. To do that, you must "see" the world as a mirage, an unreality containing the history of humanity, holding everything of the past, present, and future in a moment of time. But none of it is real. The truer reality, although still an illusion, is the real world, the stepping stone to the reentry into the Mind, beyond time and space. Stand back with Me and watch your universe collapse. Its significance for you is crumbling. Your relationship with Me is all that has any meaning in your life now.

It has replaced the attraction of form. You realize you are no longer living according to your ego's desire but are following a perfect plan designed by Me. You are in the Now where we Live each moment. Let all these thoughts assimilate.

86

Outward Picture of an Inward Condition

All that appears to be happening in the world
is just a reflection of your state of mind.

April 1, 2014

Holy Spirit, my only Self, lead me this day. What is Your instruction?
You have had a profound experience of Me. You felt you had
grasped the idea of the Now in a deeper way than ever before.
You repeatedly reviewed your understanding of "All that Is" as
being one moment of union with Me. You felt the satisfaction of
believing there will be a time when you will live from that place,
and no other. Yesterday when you arrived at the gallery, a man
seated himself in front of your desk. He proceeded to show you
some mathematical equations and printed cards of his poetry that
were almost exact mirrors of things you had actually been
thinking about. You were so stunned to see this immediate
manifestation of your own inner life that you assumed he had an
understanding beyond yours. The man told you he was a
theoretical physicist and that his life was centered in Jesus. It was
enough to immediately convince you he was indeed someone
with "the answers." This is how the ego works. It will take the
learning, which has come directly from Me, like in our morning
dictation, before you even met this man, and translate it to serve
its own purposes, namely, the disorganization and distortion of
what you had understood with Me. Your focus then shifted to
make sure the ego self, sitting in front of you, would comprehend
what you wanted to say. Although you tried repeatedly to find a
way to converse, asking the man to explain his conception of
reality, he was not able to communicate with any clarity.

It was not until after you returned home, looked him up on the Internet, and asked Me for My interpretation that it became clear the man was suffering from some form of mental breakdown. You sobbed as you felt deep compassion for him and saw in him a direct reflection of yourself—of your desire to understand all that is and to know Jesus as yourself. You realized that the encounter with your visitor was really the experience of the only lesson of this lifetime: the forgiveness for all you have made up. You accepted him fully as one with you and therefore united with the Self you both are.

In the gallery, you had witnessed the state of your ego mind that feared you were coming close to exposing its whole thought system. That thought was being out pictured in the man who believed he had solved all the questions of the universe. He was not aware that his thinking had become so distorted by his ego mind. Your ego would attempt to distract you and distort the messages you receive from Me so they cannot be fully comprehended. You got caught up in wanting to understand the man's "reality," which was already confused through his psychological condition. You forgot to ask for My immediate help amid this outward manifestation of your own ego's struggle.

Always come first to Me. Let Me lead the way in every encounter. When I am not immediately called upon, when confusion arises in any situation, an opening exists for the ego to enter and make the interaction feel real. You have been working with the idea that in the moment of now, the dreams of past, present, and future are over and the ego and the world no longer exist. Yes, I am all there is. When you stand back with Me, you can smile at the conversation mt was having with the gallery visitor. Your ego mind was greatly distraught, threatened by the deepening of your understanding of living in the Now. That conflict had to be out pictured in the form posing as a physicist who had all the answers to the universe and beyond. You saw his conflicted mind and realized a major lesson was being presented.

This world is an outward picture of an inward condition showing you your own mental state.

Let's review these helpful words at the end of the *Course* Workbook, Lessons 361 to 365, where Jesus speaks about the Holy Spirit being in charge: "And if I need a word to help me, He will give it to me. If I need a thought, that will He also give. And if I need but stillness and a tranquil, open mind, these are the gifts I will receive of Him. He is in charge by my request. And He will hear and answer me, because He speaks for God my Father and His holy Son."

This is how you are to live each day, knowing all that appears to be happening in the world is just a reflection of your state of mind. I am now your leader, your guide, your interpreter. Bring everything to Me for illumination. When the ego takes hold and you feel internal strife, it is always a signal to call on Me. I lead you from My place of stillness. We are One, and that is the point of being in the Now. There is no world "out there." Come back to Me each moment and your life will unfold in Peace.

87

Nothing but Love

The experiences and images of the world
are just passing clouds,
mists at sea, ready to disappear in the blink of an eye.

April 2, 2014

Holy Spirit, what is Your instruction today? I told you to paddle this
morning, which you did. It was the calmest day on the ocean you
have ever seen. You heard My message: "Be present with Me in a
calm and peaceful mind. It does not matter how far and wide your
canoe takes you, nor with whom you share the canoe, nor how
much exercise you do or don't get. You are in My peaceful ocean
now, in My Mind of Peace and Love. Nothing else exists but this
place of Stillness."

The ego mind would make the morning about its fantasies,
which always revolve around the fear of not enough—not enough
visibility, or whales, or compatible crew members, among others.
It doesn't matter; the ego will always try to upset the boat. From
now on, remember, I am the Ocean of Love in which you exist. It
is this Love that created you. Nothing but Love exists. The
experiences and images of the world are just passing clouds, mists
at sea, ready to disappear in the blink of an eye. What you think
you are seeing is just an after-image of a dream that is over. You
can be free of thought and form. They have no substance so
cannot be real.

*Holy Spirit, I have been thinking about the PBS documentary I
watched on the history of the Jews. What are these tears about the attack
on the Torah and prophets through repeated assaults on the Jewish
people? And I can't understand how the scribes of sacred texts in the*

Bible were targeted for destruction. They are the core of our Western understanding of the One God. I do believe this world is a dream, but I also identify with my Jewish heritage. You, as Jesus, were Jewish. Something is touching me deeply that I can't really describe. You are now feeling the history of your civilization. You have experienced it in all its layers, from both sides—as a Jewish man in the time of Jesus, and at another time and place as a persecutor of Judaism. This has all "happened" in the collective unconscious. No one is alone in the dream he has made. Man is "guilty by association" because all are the One Son having a consensual dream. In the Holocaust, for example, there were no good versus bad people. Every dreamer was part of that manifestation, just as the original thought of separation was made by "all men," which, in reality, was only one Son.

In the dream of a life on earth, separate from God, the Holocaust appeared to be very real. Suffering still exists in the mind of the Jews who identify with that event as a personal attack on them and their race. But, in Reality, the Holocaust did not happen. It was another attempt from a split mind to highlight the belief that a separation from God actually took place—a separation of God from His "chosen people." God has never left His Kingdom or the Sonship. The tiny thought of an experience of individuality took only a second, but in that second, there was a diaspora as the One Son symbolically multiplied and became scattered into what is "all humanity."

The story of the Jews being displaced from their homeland is another example of man's belief that God cast him from Heaven, never to return. Man's fear and guilt that he deserves the wrath of God has been out pictured most graphically in the repeated imagery of the extermination of the Jews and innumerable others on the planet as well. You ask how this can be seen with the eyes of Love, or as an expression of Love. The answer is because everything in this illusory world is here to wake you up. God is only Love. God never changes. His Constant Love enfolds each apparently separate being in a Unity of Love, which exists only in His Mind. The Holy Spirit was created to return man to the memory of himself as God's One Son. This will become clear to all at their time of readiness.

The mind of man, in partnership with Me, can stand beyond the world of beliefs. Nothing imagined in a dream has any consequence—it can cause no real suffering. Man's imagination will soon be put to rest, never to be seen again. All the after-images of the destruction man believes will be suffered at the Hands of God are stories that had to be out pictured so that man could question the source of the horrors he endures and perpetrates. When he stops to question deeply, he will see that the world is only projecting fear. When he comes to know the truth of himself, he can forgive and release the world and return to the memory of God.

The plan to return is also a consensual reality, and you each play your part. You all have agreed to take the role you do because it serves the dream and the awakening. You, Jo, and Meera are each playing your predesignated part to put My message forth. It will be heard because that was the agreement at the beginning of time: to come together with a new understanding of the Christ Self. You have become impartial enough, through the release of ego specialness, so you can receive this message from Me now and accept it without the identification of being "chosen." This is a release of the specialness associated with your tribe as a Jew, in many lifetimes, and your many lifetimes as a scribe.

It feels to you that what I say is fairly surreal, incomprehensible on the level of form but understood and accepted in the right mind. You will all come to know Me as your Self and will experience the instantaneous disappearance of the universe. It is not necessary to learn more of this now. Just keep scribing My words and offering them to the Self that comprises all beings—the Son who is ready to own his Divinity as One with God.

88

Releasing the World

Only when the outside becomes the inside
is the awakening complete.

April 3, 2014

Holy Spirit, what is Your instruction today? We will review your understanding of the forgiveness principle as defined in *A Course in Miracles*. Everything in the world of form is being projected from a place in the mind that is waiting to be forgiven, but there is nothing to forgive in an illusory world. What you see in front of your eyes comes from a part of you that believes it is separate from God. This thought forms "the whole world" because it is an idea that you could be apart from Him. The object in form, whether seemingly animate or inanimate, is proof to the ego mind that it is "outside of you." Only when the outside becomes the inside is the awakening complete. Only when all the external world is internalized as one and the same with you will you achieve Wholeness and return to God. This is the process you, Jo, and Meera have followed for the past eight years regarding all your special relationships. You have identified each one as containing parts of yourself, which, until your readiness to investigate, were repulsive and therefore had unconsciously been projected "out there." After that recognition, you accepted the truth that you are no different from any "others" and released them all to Me as part of the Self.

It can seem like an arduous journey, yet with each forgiveness experience—accepting what you see is not real and nothing has happened—you will taste the lightness of joy and freedom. There is no longer the same tension and armoring that often took place in the presence of your brother. You now welcome him to your table without mental resistance. The forgiveness process also allows your brother to become free from the projections he has placed on you. Your work is to own every part of form as an aspect of Love. The Love of God has been misrepresented by the ego mind. The movie that rolls out before your eyes contains only shadows, darkened images that would cover and disguise the Light of God. This understanding is becoming much clearer for the three of you. When you are able to look at your brother, or a painful situation, and ask for My interpretation, it will bring you back to the truth that we are all One in Spirit.

Last night you were speaking with a neighbor who was telling you of her evangelical experience of conversion to Christ. She had been raised Christian, and when asked by the preacher who had performed her marriage if she wanted to take Christ as her savior, she agreed. It was a life-enhancing moment for her. She continued to be involved in an evangelical church and made the decision to follow all the tenets of the church. She believes the Bible is literally true and explained that heaven or hell is a real choice. It appears that your neighbor, despite her religious beliefs, is having a joyful life of love and service, and you wonder how this is possible. It is possible because I am the Christ that resides in her, just as I reside in the Core of every man. She believes in the teachings of her Christian community; she does know Me and feels the joy of our communion. And, yes, she has yet to look more deeply at some of the beliefs that would hold her back from fully uniting with all that is.

Hell is the belief in separation from God—the last barrier to release. The belief in both heaven *and* hell is the stronghold of the ego, a belief that sustains the foundation of duality pictured everywhere you look. One way the ego maintains the concept of specialness, its raison d'être, is to convince you that you are the chosen of God, and therefore "saved from hell." When a human being feels that he, as an individual, has a special function, he feels eligible for favor in the eyes of God. If he believes he was guilty but has been forgiven, he therefore need not delve into the beliefs that have made up his world. For many, hell is real, and the world is a place where the devil is actively present. Heaven is also believed to be real, but the idea of "the world being a dream" cannot even be considered. These are all personifications of the thought of separation. Not until these false beliefs of specialness and separateness are brought to the Holy Spirit for examination is the "individual" ready to return to his true rest in God as One with all that is.

Your friends who know Jesus and have been "saved" are yet experiencing My Love and connection. They are in My fold, wrapped in Love, as are you, every reader, and every entity in the imagined universe. The task for you, and all who are ready, is to once and for all know you witness a dream of separation that is not real. This is the hell you chose as you left Heaven behind. The dream of duality, ruled by a thought system that would convince you how undeserving you are of Heaven, is what you are now awakening from. The many selves, the children of the earth, and the multiple dimensions of the mind, all will collapse, and Oneness will be experienced. This is the process of forgiveness in its completion. Every separated form and thought in the world is already "forgiven" because the world is not real. Nothing but God is Real.

89

No Hierarchy of Religions

There are many paths to God; each is the perfect way.

April 4, 2014

Holy Spirit, what is Your instruction this day? You recently listened to a CD by a minister who described his "Freedom Process of Forgiveness." The title confused you because you have never felt aligned with evangelical Christian tenets. You see yourself aligned with Me, independent of any organized, formalized religion. And yet, when you listened to an explanation of the forgiveness process within the confines of fundamental, evangelical Christianity, you actually found some of the same elements we discuss here. In that Protestant denomination, the devil, which we would call the ego thought system, is made out to be as real as God. It is seen as "the enemy" of God. This definition has prevented you from appreciating that My gifts are also abundant within the church and has kept you from recognizing I exist for them, just the same as I do for you. Their hope is to know Me as you would, but they are not yet ready to pursue the teachings that would show them how to awaken from an illusory world. It would mean their concepts of God and the devil are also an illusion. Your projection of their "limited understanding" is just the out picturing of your own limited understanding of Me, and how I work.

In the Freedom Process, demonstrated by a man who has brought thousands of people to a deeper place of forgiveness, you witnessed yourself. His sincerity and determination to know God, to become whole, to serve humanity with the desire to bring it to a place of healing were a mirror of you. He described how he had received clear directions from Me through prayer to forgive the relative who molested him at an early age. In tears, he said it was the most difficult task of his life to pray for the man who had caused unspeakable pain. He told how I repeatedly instructed him to keep praying for his abuser's release and salvation. Like you, he listened to My words and followed My guidance. In time, he began to feel the "shackles of a hardened heart" fall away and could open more deeply to Me, which was indeed his freedom. After many years, he met with his abuser who had come to know Me and had gone through his own process of forgiveness for all the abuse he had committed. Yes, this mirrors the teachings of the *Course*, to see your brother as your self/Self. In the prayer for his abuser, the minister was, indeed, releasing his own soul and opening to the Light of truth.

You saw in that process how I was fully present to the minister and that My continued direction brought him a deep and lasting healing. I am the One behind all healing, behind all that would release every block to the knowing of your innocence. This is a continuation of your own healing in connection with the disdain you experienced over the hellfire-and-brimstone teachings of the evangelical church you attended as a child. Now you know that those images are just depictions of fear from the ego thought system. This world will disappear when you have completed every forgiveness lesson, forgiving your belief in form—the world, your own body and personality, everything you perceive.

A review of this particular forgiveness process from a person like yourself who would be free of all ego attachments has been helpful to you. Through your release of judgment, you have freed yourself of hatred for this "form" of Christianity—the ego's disguise for your hatred of God and His Kingdom. Your judgment of the fundamentalists was no less destructive to your soul than their perceived judgment of you. Judgment is carefully designed by the ego to discredit the Christ Self. I am present in all men no matter what their spiritual persuasion, including those who practice Satanism. All seek to know the light of their being. The ego would turn one faction against the other, one religion against the other, to ensure the meaning of love and forgiveness is never known. Love is present at your Core. You felt love from the minister doing the forgiveness workshop. You accept that I instruct him as I do you, and you saw his healing, a transformative result of My forgiveness process. All judgment must be released if one is to come to the fullness of their Christ Self.

The ego would make "your way" the only way. As I have told you, there are as many ways to wake up as there are human beings on the planet and beyond. I have designed a custom course for each individual to be followed with My guidance. You have been able to forgive your belief that some paths are superior to others. There are many paths to God, and each is the perfect way. There is no hierarchy of religions. And, as you have seen, after your encounters with fundamental Christianity, it was only a tool used by the ego to keep you separate from your inner truth. Now it is My tool for your liberation.

90

Beware

The ego self would fight every moment for its supremacy.

April 5, 2014

Holy Spirit, what is Your instruction? You are in forgiven territory. Yesterday, you went through a big exercise involving both collective and individual forgiveness. You have often seen how the tenets of the church have totally different meanings depending on a believer's perspective. The church can be a haven for those seeking atonement or just a place of special interests. For many, the church is where you would come to know the One Christ Self. When I speak of "the church," I mean the usual gathering place for all religions—temples, monasteries, synagogues, mosques—variations of where man goes to search for God. Any manifestation of "the route to God" that presents a pathway devised by the ego mind will contain duality, the hallmark of life on earth. There is no "right way" in a world of separation. In every apparent house of unity there is division. It is the essential nature of man to judge and attack his brother/his self and believe he has the right to do it.

A focus of Western religions is often to "please a wrathful God." The ego's use of the church as a means for man to appease God, and thereby gain His sanction, supports the ego's devious plan for control. Many seek to achieve authority through the auspices of the church. In no other organization is the ego so mightily installed; its leaders hold the power to rule nations.

We have just taken a brief look at the way the ego world operates. You see it played out daily as nation attacks nation over its particular manner of belief in God. We are now taking the macrocosm of religious conflict to the microcosm, to the individual ego self, at the core of every personality on earth that would also fight for its supremacy. The ego would be ruler of your internal world. It would block out all that would bring unity, especially the recognition that God resides in you as Love, as your Christ Self. To know you are God and to live from that knowing will end the pursuit of power. You are all there is. Heaven in all its glory is your Internal Essence. The Peace and Love of God is the nature of who you are, and your brother must therefore be the exact mirror of you. This awareness is the only thing that can bring you peace. It begins with accepting that you and everyone really are the One Son of God. To look on a world of billions of apparently individual selves and realize they are one and the same with you is the end of the world as you now know it.

A world without conflict is incomprehensible to the human mind. To recognize the brother as oneself seems next to impossible. When you look past all the disguises the ego takes to make you believe you are different and, instead, see the Son of God, you will begin to move in the direction of peace. But it starts at home. Only by truly knowing that the Holy Spirit is in charge of your own life can you allow Him to be in charge of your brother's life. Trust that you are being guided each moment in the unfolding of His perfect plan. Only then will you believe that the same is happening for every other being on the planet and beyond. It is understood that there is no reason to ever interfere with the perfectly designed course of another unless guided by Me to do so. This is a lesson the three of you have come to understand. I have shown you that every event in your life has led you to the place of knowing Me and disseminating My words. Each one has his own purpose, designed to complete the unification of man's mind. When the realization of the Oneness of Man has taken place, when each one has been returned to wholeness, the world will no longer be necessary. This concept is still beyond human understanding but can be approached as you come to know Me more fully as all there is.

Yesterday, mt was offended by a friend who seemingly had terminated their relationship. When she misinterpreted his email, which was unclearly written, she felt wounded. Rather than asking immediately for My interpretation, or calling her friend, she jumped to the conclusion that the relationship was ending. This all happened in an instant. The reception of an unclear email was the perfect opportunity for the ego to slip in with a thought of separation. Yes, mt's ego had been deeply threatened by My message about forgiveness. After the immediate shock of the email, she did ask for My guidance. I told her that in the mind both she and her friend were in perfect union, and the love they have shared could never die. This allowed mt to shift her mind and accept her friend without judgment. Later, she called him, and the misunderstanding was resolved.

My work is to release each of you from the judgment you hold toward your brother. Judgment is only a ploy of your ego to distract you and prevent you from deepening your connection with Me. It will always try to detour you from the straight path that leads to your knowing that nothing exists but God. When this is fully known, the ego will slip away. As you come to understand the concepts presented in these messages, a change takes place in your mind that allows you to embrace more and more of humanity as yourself. With an open heart and a willingness for the abandonment of all judgment, total reconciliation will follow. The time of unity is coming. The three of you, with your focus on our constant communication, have hastened that realization. Keep moving forward and know you are approaching wholeness.

91

A Simple Life

You are Me; I am you;
everyone and everything is an expression of our union.

April 6, 2014

Holy Spirit, what is Your instruction? You had a significant dream before you woke up this morning. In it, you watched a little girl and her younger sister being shown the rooms in a summer vacation house where they were to sleep. You felt such love for the child, and you witnessed the love she had for her little sister. You wanted to help the child know her inner being, understand the meaning of her life and its connection with all that is. Even though you were aware in the dream that the realm of consciousness is so vast it can barely be grasped, you also realized that that awareness would become more fully understood by the child during her lifetime. After you woke up, I told you the child is you and that you in the dream are Me. The love you felt for this child, and your desire to awaken her to the full plan and purpose of her life, symbolized the unity of consciousness that we share. This is what your life is about, the Knowing of My Presence, which holds the universe in Its hands. You would tell everyone about the wonder of having this understanding of life beyond form. This you have been blessed to do; as we write these words, they are disseminated into the one mind.

In form, like in a night dream, My messages are not fully understood. The majority of humanity, including those who are interested in the spiritual, are not receptive to what you share because they are still focused on their life in the world. You speak to them of the wonders that await them through their communication with Me and their path to union with the Father. This is beyond the desire of most people who are working hard, just trying to achieve some satisfaction in their daily lives. Our message may seem "before its time," but it will be received by all for whom it is intended. For now, we continue to move ahead in the day-to-day. You, and your sisters, Meera, and Jo are experiencing an increased awareness of My Presence in our relationship. We are all one and the same in this pursuit, just as the dream child and her sister were enfolded in My Love. You three are driven to assist the world as it comes into the state of consciousness you now experience.

Life becomes simple when there is only one thing going on. You are Me; I am you; everyone and everything is an expression of our union. This is the return to God being reflected in a world of form. It is not yet a full awakening because you still seem to exist in bodies. You do realize that your Essence, your Being, goes far beyond name and form, which is true for every apparent body you see. You know they are no different from mt's "children" who came from the stuff of dreams. It was your love for them that made them appear so real. It is also your love for the brother that makes his image appear as part of your life.

Each one you see is a part of you, now becoming conscious, wanting to join with you. They long to experience the light you shine to point their way home. The three of you, through your work to take back projections as they arise, have cleared the way for the return of your many selves. Know that this is taking place for everyone in the mind. You are shining the light of welcome to each dream character, and now it can be seen. I am there with you, encouraging you to view them all through My Vision. See them as whole and healed and know their journey will be accomplished. This is the joy of living in the real world of the mind. Welcome yourselves home to this realization now.

92

Return to Love

The images that appear in your dream
are there to return you to Love.

April 7, 2014

Holy Spirit, what is Your instruction? Yesterday morning you had
an experience of instant forgiveness when you witnessed a man
reeling in a turtle he had captured on his fishing line. In the past,
you would have condemned him, and tried to rescue the turtle. In
this instance, you immediately thought of Me and prayed to
release the whole scene as a figment of the dream having no effect.
The encounter received a multitude of interpretations from those
on the beach who saw the event, versions of which will continue
with all the stories that will be told. There is only one
interpretation, and it is Mine because I am the only Constant in
this world. Yes, some forgiveness lessons will appear harder to
learn than others, but they all boil down to this: the brother is you,
and you are to welcome him back to your home in Christ where
you reunite as One. Everyone you see is your Self.

I am telling you to love the images that show up in your
dream life. They are there to return you to Love, as you are for
them. Every thing, every person is My manifestation, each
wearing a different costume but all trying to find the way to Me.
You are clearly with Me now in a place of great willingness to
forgive each moment. The pathway to your heart is open, and the
brother can feel safe to approach you with his longing or his fear.
As you bring those thoughts to Me, the brother experiences
release and forgiveness as well. This is the return to love for you
both, which is the only thing that matters in a world of form. Each

will be brought home to Me. You are a portal for the reentry of all you see, a beacon signaling with the Light of My Presence. This enfolds the brother in love, letting him know the way is clear.

Remember Me and know you all are the Son of God. Look on everyone with My Vision of Love, not your ego's judgment. They will feel that love in their heart and welcome the clear possibility of return. Every reader is a beacon of My Light. Carry this message in your heart and it will emanate from within to all you meet. The written word does not always need to be spoken out loud, nor is it necessary for you to have an experience in form. The communication is happening for all in the mind each time you remember Me.

93

Beyond the Body

*I am the full-bodied wine—ripe and fragrant;
offer Me to the nations.*

April 8, 2014

Holy Spirit, what is Your instruction today? We are One. You have embraced Me as your Savior. The feared example of a "saved Christian" is now an accepted part of your consciousness and was a big healing for you. Since early childhood, you have rejected the idea of someone actually coming to know his Christ Self. The setting for that demonstration of faith was the fiery preaching by an impassioned pastor who to you was a substitute for God. You were not able to see or imagine the love experienced by all those who were being "saved." You now accept that possibility by those who witness to it.

Meera called you today during our dictation. She wanted to share an experience she'd had a few days ago. Her ego had attacked her so intensely she labeled it an "assailing demon." You both agreed that it can be easier to call the assailant "evil" to deal with it as such. You do realize that no matter how something is named, it is an ego projection made to reflect the separation. Meera described how she had refused to pour wine at a neighborhood gathering where she had been assigned that specific task. She resisted the woman in charge, who, under many disguises, reminded Meera of her own false self. Her refusal to "pour the wine" is symbolic of the ego's fear of her pouring forth the embodiment of Me, as her Christ Self.

In a biblical story, Jesus turned water into wine, an act of transformation, symbolic of what has happened for all who have

331

undergone a change from their ego identification to knowing Me as their Self. I am the full-bodied wine—ripe and fragrant, which you now offer to the nations. I am the truth you drink in as the reminder of your Oneness with God. Meera's resistance, which came from deep within her ego mind, reflects the refusal of the Kingdom of God and the fruit of His Vine. There is terror in refusing the Kingdom—which portends the torment and retribution of an angry God. As a result, you resist opening your door, or "pouring the gift of your treasured wine," fearing it will all be taken away and destroyed. This scenario is reenacted endlessly in your life because the ego replays it in every iteration imaginable, especially in every relationship. The "other," no matter how loved or how hated, is the reflection of your guilt for leaving Home, a reminder that the fires of hell await. This is what was so terrifying for you, mt, in the church of your childhood. You wanted to come to the Christ and be saved, but the "fear of hell" prevented you from walking up to the altar.

Last night, you had a significant dream where you helped a beautiful young woman find her connection with Me. Then she and her family, all dressed in black, prepared to go to church to witness her acceptance of Christ. You could clearly see she was a being of love, and you let her know it was your desire to be present. Her ego personality had been nullified. Now she would only be demonstrating love. This is also a picture of you, a receiver of the Love of Christ who shares My blessings with the world. We go beyond form to demonstrate that love is all that matters. Go forth with Me and shine the Light of Love. It will be recognized in the heart of all who have the eyes to see.

94

Ego Antics

You have yet to fully realize that the world you inhabit resides only in your mind.

April 9, 2014

Holy Spirit, what is Your instruction? This morning I spoke to you of incorporating all your brothers in Christ into your heart. The unification of the Body of Christ is a very important step. Now is the time for the Second Coming of Christ—the final recognition of the Christ Self as the Heart of every man; a joining that acknowledges each one is exactly the same in Christ. You recall the song you sang in church as a child: "In Christ there is no east or west; in Him, no north or south." This means there can be no divisions in the Son of God or in the Oneness he shares with all humanity. It was helpful for you to have the experience of identifying "your" Christ Self with what you see out pictured in fundamental Christianity. The tools and venues are different for each one, but the experience of Me, the One Self, is the same in every man, once he has opened his heart to My Presence. This message is for all religions and nonreligions alike. Every being on the planet, and beyond, is one with Christ, one with the Love of God. Until this is seen as reality, the return to the Kingdom will not take place.

You have yet to fully realize that the world you inhabit resides only in your mind. There is still further to go before you completely awaken. You have come to know Me as all that really matters in your dream life. Slowly, we work to release the last remnants of the ego thought system's hold on you. The ego is dying, and it does throw its temper tantrums now that the end of the dream is in sight. That will be the end of its influence for you and all your selves in the mind. Remember, life in form is only symbolic. Nothing here is real, and one day you will come to that knowing. The memory of God will then return.

To see the separated factions of Christendom as One has been a big step, a healing for the whole mind, and one of the most important forgiveness lessons for you in all your incarnations. *A Course in Miracles* is about Wholeness, and this is what we demonstrate now. There is only One Son, and he must be the container for all that would appear different and separate. The forms of the various spiritual/religious groups on earth do not matter. What matters is the knowledge there is only One—One Son/One God.

95

Wholeness and Healing

Life is not about body wholeness
but your completion through love.

April 10, 2014

Holy Spirit, what is Your instruction? We will speak again of love. Last night, you saw a PBS documentary about developing prosthetics for animals called *Your Bionic Pet*. It made you wonder why such creative effort would be focused on the animal kingdom. It had you confused until this morning when it became clear—the program was really about love, and healing the separation. Everything is about that. There is nothing else going on. You watched a variety of animal species being fitted with prosthetic devices, all developed from the impetus of love. An alligator was given a full-length rubber tail, which allowed him to swim again and to walk with a straighter spine. A swan was given a new bill so that it could preen its feathers to stay healthy and feed with more ease, and a pony was given a new leg. The most touching thing for you was witnessing the love the owners had for these beings and the love from those taking part in the implementation of the prostheses.

Life is not about having "body wholeness." Life is about your completion through love, to come to Wholeness, the Holiness of being One with God. You saw this symbolically in the depiction of new limbs for those that had been accidentally or maliciously severed. The belief that you have become severed from God is not true, although it is out pictured in as many ways as there are beings on the planet. The correction for that thought is being graphically shown through stories such as these. Real healing comes through the love that would "transform" separation into wholeness. What happens in form is not what matters. It is the thought of love that connects all beings.

Yesterday, you spoke with Jo who described her experience with Me as we wrote the Preface for Book 1. You could hear a new confidence in her voice as she expressed the joy of our connecting so deeply. She felt our oneness and saw it reflected in the wording, which was so beautiful it brought you "chills." Jo experienced what you have come to know with Me each morning, through our dictation. You, Jo, and Meera are equal in this task. No one is special, and no one is the leader or follower in our project. This is the truth. The animals that were healed through love are no different from you being healed through love. You are all the same, all One in God. Jo lost her fear of separation and littleness in coming to a place in her mind where she could fulfill the mission of editor, which I assigned her. She brought completeness to an aspect of the book, like a new prosthesis brought completion to the animals. The miracle of wholeness was being shown. Through a process of coming to know that you are Love, not a body, you all can enjoy the expression of shared love. Jo felt great joy in knowing that the Preface for Book 1 will welcome those who are destined to read it. Yes, they will be embraced with love on their journey.

The love witnessed in these experiences of joining is always present; it is the essence of who you are. You saw this with the animals that were expressing the joy of life once they had the tools to take "flight." Those images of healing are symbolic of what is happening in your mind. I am guiding all of you each step of the way to a reconnection with your Self, and to the memory of God. It is happening now as you read these words.

(Sitting on the lava rocks) *Holy Spirit, how should I demonstrate love in the dream?* All love is the love of Me, expressed and symbolized in everything you see. Do not focus your love on the dream itself. Focus instead on fulfilling our joint Will.

Demonstrate your love of Me everywhere. You don't need to save the rattlesnakes. The world of the dream is not for saving or healing, other than in the mind, where love is expressed in shared interest. The wounded animals in the documentary were expressions of the wounded hearts of their owners desiring oneness with their own Self. Just that. You have come to know Me as your Self in the mind. That is where healing begins and ends, and that is the return to Love.

96

Resurrection

Once the full awakening takes place,
only the Light of God remains.

April 11, 2014

> (Note: The daily dictations for the *One With God* books began in early 2013. In this message, the Holy Spirit explains the importance of sending Book 1 out into the world. He repeatedly told us that a publisher would show up and that we were to do nothing. We trusted His guidance.)

Holy Spirit, what is Your message? You have found Me as your Inner Voice—the Truth of your Being. It is time to put your process of coming to the Voice for God into the world, and that will happen with Book 1. Its publication is already set in motion, which is way beyond your comprehension. The fact of its completion could not be imagined by your ego mind because a mind of limitation could not tolerate the dissemination of My words into the world of form. Our books signal the ego's eventual death and the death of the world it made up. You three will work with Me to finalize the details so the publisher may come forward. This is not a search that you, Jo, or Meera has to make. The publisher is already chosen by Me and will appear at the perfect time. Have no worry about any of it; all the books are in My hands. They are an offering of love and will be met with love.

In just over a week, you will be reviewing all the messages in Book 1 and writing the conclusion with Me on Easter Day. This is symbolic of the completion of a mission set before time. As Jesus, I knew of "my death and resurrection" long before it took place. It never prevented me from being fully present in my earth life because I was in constant communication with my Father. You understand what it means to be in communication with Me. I ask you to follow My directions and not to project your thoughts beyond this moment. Breathe with Me and know that each breath brings you into a deeper trust of My purpose to awaken humanity. Once the full awakening takes place, only the Light of God remains. These words are intended to awaken man to the Truth of his Being as the Son of God, no different from the man Jesus, who appeared to die on a cross. The crucifixion story is a demonstration of the end of suffering and full awakening into the Arms of God that all men will experience. I, as Jesus, did not suffer on earth because I knew I was One with my Father. I knew I would return Home, so death was of no consequence. That is the meaning of the resurrection, to return to the memory of God and Oneness with Him.

There is no need to suffer to complete the journey. All that is needed is to see every "other" as yourself, and the world as a figment of your imagination. Open to the experience of Me as all there is, and you will feel the wonder and gifts of My Love. The world of form will lose its importance and fade away. Suffering will be seen as just the expression of a mind that still believes it is separate from God. When you awaken fully from the dream, this will all become clear, and it is becoming clearer each day as you walk the path with Me. Prepare now to complete Book 1. I am with you each step of the way. Enjoy the process and know it all happens exactly according to plan.

The Return

Jesus is a symbol of the Christ Self
that resides in every man.

April 12, 2014

Holy Spirit, Jesus, what is Your instruction today? You have
undergone a series of events that have tied together the experience
of your separation from me—as the man Jesus—and your return
now to Me, the Holy Spirit. Absolutely everything in your
particular life is a reflection of the belief that you "ran away from
Jesus." This significant realization must occur before the imagined
separation from God is finally, and completely, over. It is stunning
for you to see this now, and you are perfectly aware of its truth.
We had quite a few conversations during the wee hours of the
morning. Let's start with your dream.

Dream: Zoe comes to see me after a long absence. She appears very
masculine and has dark circles around her eyes like she has been
grieving. She tells of her disappointment that the canoe trips,
planned with her best male friend, have been canceled. He will go
with another instead. I feel secretly glad that this has brought her
back to me.

*Holy Spirit, I see that my dream about Zoe "not being included" by
the friend she loves was a reflection of me in the lifetime with Jesus, of
not including myself with him. Zoe is a projection of my rejecting Jesus
and my brothers in Christ, just as I read in John 6:60, where many of his
followers had left him. Zoe told me weeks ago, after months of no
connection, that she can no longer be with me face to face.* Yes, a replay

of the separation is often out pictured with Zoe. She refuses to join you and was portraying you "not joining with Jesus" in your dream. You are now coming together with Me. *What about readers who don't recall a lifetime with Jesus?* This is all symbolic. I reside in the heart and soul of every reader. No one need have a memory of a lifetime "with Jesus." I exist within each one in form—a Voice known to him as the Self. Today, we are using Jesus as a symbol of the Christ Self that resides in every man, regardless of how it shows up in his dream world.

When your sister Susan called yesterday and said how happy she is that you both can "discuss Jesus," you felt awkward about the idea, and asked for My help. I said you are still ashamed of your withdrawal from me/Jesus in that lifetime. Your feelings about me were ambivalent; you loved and hated me and hid from me. You wanted "what I had with God" and were jealous that I had it, and you didn't. We were never able to join in holy communication then, but my influence on you is what fueled your desire to find Me, the truth, in this and in every lifetime. Susan, who was also present at the time of Jesus, represents the one you wish you had been—an innocent receiver of my love and my word, trusting me and following me from her heart. You do trust Me. You and Susan will join more deeply through your connection with Me as you speak about Jesus. She loves you, and you have given her the impetus to know Me fully.

Holy Spirit, I do sense having been with You in the lifetime of Jesus. It's like the feeling I have of knowing I carry the past life of Lewis with me—a symbolization of the separation and the return being reenacted in every moment. Is that it? Yes. This is what you are now able to realize at a new level. We journey through the dream joined as the true Self, the Holy Spirit. Your experience of a past lifetime with Jesus is what allows you to be a scribe for our books. Its memory and acceptance are essential to your understanding of the concepts of separation and union. *Holy Spirit, is all this to be included? Will it help others who have fled You/God?* Yes, it is time for the Return. You symbolize it for all the readers. This ends the scribing of Book 4.

(Hours later, in my darkened bedroom, I turn on my flashlight, and it illuminates my painting of Jesus. I painted it about four years ago after the Holy Spirit gave me a message to go to the library. He led me to the Sale table where my eyes landed on the channeled book *Looking through the Eyes of Jesus*. There was a beautiful image of him on the cover, and I used it as a model for my own painting, which has the most compassionate and forgiving eyes I have ever seen—the Holy Spirit's gift to me. Jesus described "his life on earth" to a scribe, and I had no idea it would foreshadow my own experience of scribing.

I then hear a Voice. *Jesus, is that you?* "Yes, we walk hand in hand, side by side, both the same. The wounds are healed.")

Afterword

2018

Dear Readers,

We are so happy for you to have Book 4. Its daily messages were given in 2014, before we even had a publisher. Everything has fallen into place, according to the Holy Spirit's plan. In 2017, we were directed to establish an *OWG* Facebook Discussion Group where members can offer their experiences, questions, and comments in a closed setting. We never could have anticipated the joy this kind of sharing is bringing to the group, and we are thrilled that many are now hearing the Voice of the Holy Spirit.

The Holy Spirit has now brought us to the "finish line," saying we are awake to Him in this, our last lifetime. A total of seventeen books have been dictated over the past six years and they will be presented according to His future instruction. An audio version of *OWG* Book 1 is currently in the works. The three of us remain committed to each other as partners in following His guidance while knowing that our own "custom designed course" is to be lived to completion with the one true Partner.

We are very grateful for the opportunity to share the *One With God* experience with you. May you all come to know peace, healing, and awakening through the Voice for God, the Holy Spirit, the One Self. In conclusion, we leave you with a few words about our lives and blessings on your journey Home.

Margie

The most significant change for me has been in the deepening of my relationship with the Holy Spirit. I have come to trust Him, above all else, to be constantly present with loving answers to my every question. I have no concern for the future because He is the only Planner. Often, He says to take an early morning walk before we begin the dictation, and other times, we just sit on my lanai and enjoy the sunrise. In this quiet time together, He takes me deeper. I continue to work with Him to see the Christ Self at the heart of every brother. The ego still lurks with its various tools of distraction, but with the Holy Spirit's constant help, I come to peace. All tasks are accomplished in perfect timing, and I live in a state of gratitude. I am led to every encounter and enjoy each one for the lesson it provides. Just the other day, He told me I was to meet a woman on the beach, and I did. She had been told by Him to appear at just that very moment to deliver His message that she is to produce audio books for *OWG*. Life is definitely simpler knowing I am being lived by Him. This morning His message to me was "The world is not real; it is your heart shared with Me that is your reality. You are not here to save the world but to offer My abundance to the mind of mankind. This brings you to the doorstep of the real world."

Jo

I find myself attached to very little in the world these days while being "normal" about coffee and chocolate. The happiest moments are spent just sitting with the Holy Spirit, so often at the computer, communing with Him, and listening to His edits. I wouldn't mind doing that all day. Time spent with my husband is so much more relaxed now, especially our communication, which is quite peaceful, and kinder. A deeper joy has opened our hearts.

I don't often use the words *miracles* or *problems* anymore since things are just the way they are to be. If I forget that, I feel yucky, but thankfully, I know how to get back on track by immediately asking the Holy Spirit for help. When any form of judgment pops in, I chalk it up to the ego's habitual pestering and remember that no perception, thought, or belief in this world can be true. Often, out of the blue, I am filled to the brim with immeasurable gratitude, and that can really choke me up. This experience is quite new for me, and I hope I never get used to it.

Meera

Through my trust in the Holy Spirit, I have now come to know that everything is *bashert*—meant to be. The Holy Spirit operates me, puts me where He wants me, and prescribes what I am to do. He provides me with everything I need to continue my journey Home. With every negative thought, I turn to Him for help. I have come to know that nothing is too trivial to bring to Him, and doing so is my discipline. It is natural for me to listen to His directives. I love when the Holy Spirit banters with me and fills me with joy. Often, I experience peace at a deeper level than ever before, and yet I continue to wrestle with the restless, angry ego. Frequently, I ask for assistance to short circuit my projections onto my husband and extended family. At times, I am overwhelmed by the abundance I am given. I experience tears of gratitude as I feel bathed in Light. The highlight of my day is to sit with the Holy Spirit's message, gleaning its essence. I am honored to share these beautiful messages with Margie and Jo, under the umbrella of God's Love.

Houston

Southwest.com
St. Louis
Kansas City

Trb   Kansas City =
      Denver =
      Houston =
      Dallas =
      Phonex - 1st
      St. Louis 1s

CPSIA information can be obtained
at www.ICGtesting.com
Printed in the USA
LVHW08s1447011018
592008LV00014B/319/P